CW00346206

Urban Gardening

Urban Gardening

A Hong Kong Gardener's Journal

Arthur van Langenberg

Illustrations by Ip Kung Sau

Photographs by the author

The Chinese University Press

Urban Gardening: A Hong Kong Gardener's Journal
  By Arthur van Langenberg

© **The Chinese University of Hong Kong**, 2006

All rights reserved. No part of this publication may
be reproduced or transmitted in any form or by any means,
electronic or mechanical, including photocopying, recording,
or any information storage and retrieval system,
without permission in writing from
The Chinese University of Hong Kong.

ISBN 962–996–261–6

THE CHINESE UNIVERSITY PRESS
The Chinese University of Hong Kong
SHATIN, N.T., HONG KONG
Fax: +852 2603 6692
      +852 2603 7355
E-mail: cup@cuhk.edu.hk
Web-site: www.chineseupress.com

Printed in Hong Kong

Be a Gardener.
Dig a ditch. Toil and sweat.
And turn the earth upside down.
And seek the deepness.
And water plants in time.
Continue this labour.
And make sweet floods to run,
and noble and abundant fruits
to spring.
Take this food and drink,
and carry it to God
as your true worship.

—Julian of Norwich (1342–1416)

Table of Contents

Foreword

Hong Kong is far from the usual concept of a "garden city" and yet we are blessed with many wonderful gardens—public and private. Road dividers and roundabouts, podiums and car-park planters are all taken for granted. We have large recreational parks in every district, and places like the Zoological and Botanical Gardens are all available to everyone, free of charge. Best of all, they are beautifully maintained, despite what must be substantial and ever rising labour costs.

Hong Kong has numerous private parks that are open to all, including the ever-fascinating Kadoorie Farm and Botanic Garden, the new garden at the Chi Lin Nunnery 志蓮淨苑 and many more at nunneries and monasteries around the territory. And a visit to Flower Market Road and the nearby streets does not have to cost you money if you are strong-minded. How fortunate we are compared with people in many other parts of the world. Even in China everyone pays a nominal sum for admission to all public parks and gardens. The last time I went to Britain's world-famous Kew Gardens I was, perhaps naively, shocked to find the admission charge had been increased to £10 for an adult—that was the equivalent of about HK$150 at the time. Interestingly, however, admission to Edinburgh's wonderful Royal Botanic Garden is still free.

It seems that most Hong Kong people enjoy keeping their fingers in the soil. Wherever you look, especially in the older districts, people are growing plants. Roof-tops, balconies, tiny ledges and other unpromising spots are pressed into service to raise something green, possibly edible or vaguely medicinal, but most likely flowering.

The Hong Kong Gardening Society (HKGS) was founded in the mid-1980s by a group of enthusiasts with a common interest in gardening. Then as now, not all members had gardens or balconies or even windowsills where plants would flourish. But all derive enormous satisfaction from plants. HKGS serves multiple functions, providing surrogate gardening experience for some as well as providing a contact point for gardeners to share practical things like cuttings and extra seedlings. HKGS brings together people with a common love of plants and flowers by holding regular meetings at which members can share their knowledge and experience.

Members can participate in a wide range of activities throughout the year, including workshops and talks by experts, and visits to gardens and nurseries of interest around Hong Kong and further afield. The society also acts as a forum for information on everything connected with gardening in Hong Kong.

Hong Kong residents are generally unaware of the wealth of garden pleasures across the border in southern China. In recent years HKGS members have been exploring some of the wonderful gardens of Guangdong, visiting the most famous Qing Dynasty gardens as well as the more recent gardens of Shenzhen and Guangzhou's Botanical Garden, which is one of the oldest and most extensive in China. More information on HKGS can be found on the website, *www.gardeninghongkong.com*

If you enjoy the plants grown by other people it's only human to want to try your own hand at raising something green. The question is where and how to start. Arthur van Langenberg's book tells you everything you need to know from the basics of preparing the soil, to sowing seeds and transplanting seedlings to pruning trees. He tells you how to improvise, how to produce your own compost and organic pest control sprays, where to find basic supplies and tools, and the all-important topic in Hong Kong: how to save space. He is wonderfully practical and always genial in his approach to the reader. Even armchair gardeners will enjoy this book. And I can imagine homesick Hong Kongers in other parts of the world deciding to grow their own pak choi or choi sum after a few hours immersed in Arthur's pages.

Arthur's simple but thorough, illustrated instructions on the basic principles of pruning are the best you could hope to find anywhere. His explanation of plant taxonomy (he has added scientific names as well as local Cantonese names this time around) is also admirably simple and easy to follow.

I have been trying to grow plants in Hong Kong for over 40 years. Arthur's first book, *Urban Gardening in Hong Kong*, came out around the time I graduated from pots and an old cast iron bathtub to a real garden with all the tribulations and triumphs that that implies. Simply put, I don't think I could have managed without Arthur's book. It was the first user-friendly, self-help book for local gardeners.

Reading and using Arthur's first book was like having a patient and knowledgeable neighbour, who would let me make my own mistakes, but be available with good advice at all times. Every word scatters a little loam or a few fragments of dried leaves across the page. This is a real hands-on gardener speaking to kindred spirits. Who else has written so eloquently about the therapeutic value of weeding?

Over the years I have acquired more than a few reference books from countries like Malaysia, Singapore, Thailand, India, Sri Lanka and Africa—all places where tropical and sub-tropical species thrive. But I still find myself returning to Arthur's book: he has been there. However, much though I enjoyed the book and relied on it, after a while I found myself occasionally wishing for a little more information.

Now, at last, Arthur has produced his second book. It has been worth the wait. The text has been greatly expanded and the result is even better than the first, not least because he has used the same artist, Ip Kung Sau; her engaging black and white illustrations are now supplemented by new ones in colour. Arthur has also added many new photographs (all except one, his own work). And all taken in his own garden. He has followed his abiding principle, only writing about plants that he has raised himself or plants that he has closely observed at first-hand.

Urban Gardening: A Hong Kong Gardener's Journal is a triumph and it was a privilege to be allowed to preview it. I wish the book and its author every success. I have never actually met Arthur, although we have spoken on the telephone, perhaps half a dozen times at the most. But such is the camaraderie of the cabbage patch that we are firm friends. When we do finally meet, after all the many questions and answers that pass for small talk among gardeners, in between cadging cuttings of plants that they do not have, I will have one special question: what about a third book?

Jane Ram

Activities Co-ordinator
Hong Kong Gardening Society

www.gardeninghongkong.com

Foreword

As was Arthur van Langenberg's *Urban Gardening for Hong Kong* (1983) his new book is invaluable for any English speaking gardener in Hong Kong. Its charm is that it conveys so comfortably the personal voice of its author, and his vast practical experience and knowledge. Happily in this edition he has also included botanical names and he takes a much more ecologically sensitive approach and is very frank when he departs from this.

Arthur van Langenberg comes to gardening with a wisdom that the rest of us can only hope to emulate. He has learnt by doing, shows a gentle touch, and does not seem to be out to tame and subdue his garden. He presents his stories and advice with gratitude and humility that make refreshing if surprising reading, given that gardening at times can be an exasperating pastime. His description of weeding is actually endearing and defines him as that true breed of gardener who takes the time to enjoy the many tasks—and who does not take the quick-fix option but rather relish the opportunity to be in the garden. His valuable advice to gardeners on typhoons is to be found nowhere else and his strategy of "withdrawal" is essential information about how to deal with this natural phenomenon that is an inevitable part of Hong Kong gardening. I found the section on weather as pertinent now as it was when I first read it more than 20 years ago.

A useful feature of the book is that it acknowledges the variety of planting opportunities utilized in Hong Kong and that we do not all have the ideal space. He shares my admiration for local people who plant in every conceivable container and maximize the spaces they have, to produce food and beauty. Where so many of the available glossy books are dominated by sweeping lawns and massed tropical plantings, he takes us back to the more familiar home garden in its many guises.

Karen Barretto
Conservationist Gardener

Preface

Readers who are familiar with *Urban Gardening for Hong Kong* (1983) will instantly recognise the present work to be its direct offspring. A few words of explanation are necessary to explain the alteration of name and to introduce readers to the changes found in the present book. To new readers, I bid you welcome. I hope this book will open up the world of gardening for you, city living notwithstanding, and stimulate your interest in this wonderful pastime.

Over 20 years ago, there was a gaping information void about gardening in Hong Kong conditions. *Urban Gardening for Hong Kong* was a modest attempt to partly fill that gap. Surprisingly, some overseas readers of the book found it useful even in their respective countries and thought the title was a little parochial. Hence the slight unshackling of the title to make it more inclusive. The subtitle of *A Hong Kong Gardener's Journal* clearly identifies the origins of the book and its intended readers.

Why another book over 20 years later? To begin with, I was never satisfied with the first effort, but it has taken all this time to gather courage to try again. During this time, I have gained more experience in the garden as well as learned more through the many mistakes I have made along the way. Socrates said: "A wise man learns from experience; an even wiser man learns from the experience of others." I invite you to be that wiser man or woman.

A certain amount of my thinking and methods have changed, as will be evident within these pages. Although I still give first importance to common names, scientific and Chinese names are now included for all the plants featured. The scientific names should positively identify the plants, since common names may at times be haphazard. The Chinese names should open up interest among local readers. Chinese names are particularly confusing since they vary a great deal depending on dialect and region. In this regard I have been bold, and selected what I believe to be the most appropriate Cantonese names.

The present book contains almost three times as much material as the first one, but there are inevitably many omissions which some readers may find annoying, especially if their favourite plants are not included. I make no apology for this since I adhere to my principle of only including plants of which I have some personal knowledge, or which I have closely observed. Indeed all the photographs in this book were taken entirely within the confines of my own garden or its immediate environs, and all, with one exception, were taken by me.

There is a noticeable paradox that despite the huge increase in Hong Kong's population—and, therefore, in the proliferation of dwellings—more gardens are becoming available. The reason is twofold. Firstly, there has been an expansion into the suburbs with low-rise town houses, some with small gardens. Secondly, as residential blocks grow taller—up to 80 storeys—the developers are compelled to provide more open space at ground level, and sometimes, roof gardens or terraces at certain intervals. This has resulted in a greater awareness of one's environment, a greater interest in growing things and in preserving such natural treasures as our ancient banyans. Hong Kong's wonderful country parks, so ably managed by the Country and Marine Parks Authority, have furthered this interest. At the end of the day, Hong Kong itself is the greatest paradox. Who would guess that in a territory of 1092 km², packed with seven million souls, three quarters of our home is countryside? What a remarkable place we live in.

Arthur van Langenberg

December 2005

Banyans in Forbes Street—a curious phenomenon of the Hong Kong flora. See section "Ficus" for story, p. 70.

Explanatory Notes

Common name   Chinese name

Kohlrabi 芥蘭頭

Genus —— *Brassica oleracea* var. Caulorapa

Species

Variety

This is a vegetable that deserves far more attention. It is a biennial grown as an annual. It is grown for its light green, swollen globular stem which appears just above the ground and which resembles a leafy turnip. There the resemblance ends because kohlrabi is far superior in flavour and texture. A purple variety is also available. A winter vegetable, it can be sown from October through December. Like the turnip, it can be used as a catch crop towards the end of the winter vegetable season. Sow the seeds in the ground 1 cm deep, 15 cm apart each way. Put three seeds in each drill and later thin out to retain the strongest seedling to grow to maturity undisturbed. Seeds may also be sown in pans or small plastic pots for later transplantation when the seedlings are 7 cm high. As the stem swells it lifts itself off ground level, and care should be taken to build up soil around it from time to time. Pick off the lower leaves regularly. It is important not to let the plants grow old as the texture then becomes quite fibrous. Harvest when still tender—about the size of a small orange. Raw kohlrabi, cut in small strips, adds a very pleasant crunch to any salad. It may also be successfully grown in pots, one plant to a 21-cm pot.

Key to abbreviations

sp. = species
syn. = synonym
var. = variety
x = hybrid

(Also see "Plant Taxonomy: How Plants Are Named", pp. 18–19.)

Basic Gardening

Basic Gardening

The Soil

A working knowledge of the nature of soil is perhaps the most important aspect in successful gardening. Very few gardens start off with ideal soil. The challenge is to work towards attaining this perfect soil. Those of us who do this successfully, almost by intuition, are said to have "green fingers".

Soil is a mixture of mineral particles and organic matter, living and dead, the interstices containing varying amounts of air and water. A clay soil consists of very fine particles packed closely together, with little room for air and water. On the other hand, a sandy soil consists of larger particles with more spaces in between. As would be expected, clay soils drain poorly compared to the rapid drainage of sandy soils. The ideal soil is a happy medium, allowing good drainage but holding enough water to prevent rapid drying out.

The organic content of the soil is important. Humus, as organic soil matter is known, is composed of decomposing vegetable and animal material which gives good soil its dark, rich colour. Far more important than providing colour, humus makes the soil porous and friable, prevents clumping, allows for penetration of air, and holds water.

The ideal soil, or "loam", has a light, crumbly texture, is sweet-smelling, with good drainage yet able to hold the right amount of water through its high content of humus. Handling loam with your bare hands and letting it run through your fingers is a wonderful tactile sensation.

Soil Chemistry

Apart from the physical characteristics of soil, we must consider also its chemical contents, without which plants will not grow. Oxygen, carbon and hydrogen are derived from air and water, but the other nutrients must come from the soil. The three chief nutrients are nitrogen, phosphorus and potassium. Iron, calcium, magnesium and sulphur are also necessary, but in small amounts that are available in most soils. Some other elements, trace elements such as copper, zinc and boron, are also required, but in such minute quantities that we need not be concerned about them.

In the ideal conditions of nature, these nutrients are provided for by the inexorable cycle of life and death: dead animals and plants being reduced by decomposition into chemicals that feed and nurture the living through the soil. In practice, soil is seldom ideal and needs to be improved by the use of fertilisers.

There is one other important factor in soil chemistry: its reaction. Soil may be acid, alkaline or neutral. A proper pH unlocks the nutrients in fertilisers and natural breakdown products in the soil, allowing them to be optimally utilised by the plants. Most plants thrive on neutral or slightly acid soil. A few demand acid conditions and some need an alkaline soil. Alkaline soil is soil that is rich in lime. Hong Kong's soil falls mostly in this category. To reduce alkalinity peat moss and sawdust can be added to the soil. Generous watering also helps. Acid soils are common in sandy regions. Certain plants, notably rhododendrons, thrive in acid soil. Excessive acid can be easily controlled by the addition of lime. This is available in powdered form in most hardware shops.

Simple soil analysis kits are available from garden centres and can be utilised from time to time to get an idea of the chemical state of your soil. pH meters are also available and a straight readout can be had from inserting the meter into the soil.

GARDENING IS FUN

Plant Propagation

Seeds

It has been said that there is no greater demonstration of faith than a man planting seed in a field. Perhaps that is why I always feel a quiet thrill to watch the miracle of plant life emerging from a tiny dry seed. Raising plants from seeds is the simplest and cheapest method of propagation. Most plants produce seeds that eventually develop uniformly into replicas of the parent and this is especially true of many of the most popular annuals and vegetables. Many of these seeds can be collected for use the following season. Over the years, seed vendors are increasingly producing F1 hybrid seeds which result from the crossing of two strains. Hybrid seeds produce plants with some characteristics of both parents, which are usually selected because of some desirable traits in these parents. Hybrid seeds are considerably more expensive, but are usually worth the additional cost. These plants show increased vigour, uniformity and resistance to disease. However, seeds produced from hybrid plants should not be saved as the plants do not come true to type.

Most perennials can also be propagated by seeds, but some of mixed ancestry, for example, chrysanthemum, strawberries and most fruit trees, do not come true to type and are best reproduced by vegetative techniques. Still others can be raised from seed but grow slowly and do not reach maturity for a long time. These too are better propagated by other means.

Seeds vary enormously in shape and size. Each seed contains a small embryo plant that springs into life when conditions of air, moisture and warmth are provided. The seed also contains a small amount of nutrient sufficient to sustain germination and the growth of the first shoot. Always sow seeds thinly. Fine seed, such as poppy and petunia, should merely be scattered on the surface or gently pressed into the soil with a flat board. To ensure even distribution, such seed may be mixed with fine sand before sowing. Larger seed should usually be sown to a depth equal to the diameter of the seed itself. Hence a seed 5 mm in diameter should be sown 5 mm deep.

Some seeds are best sown in open ground where the plant is to grow and mature. This has the advantage that transplanting is unnecessary and that there will be no setback in the plant's growth. Excess seedlings are simply removed or "thinned". The disadvantage of this method is that the seedlings will be exposed to the elements at a vulnerable stage of their development, and this can be particularly risky in Hong Kong. For this reason, many seeds are better sown in pans or plastic pots to begin with. These can be withdrawn to safety when danger such as wind or rain threatens.

Before germination, the pans should be placed in shade. As the seedlings appear, place in increasingly better light. Keep the soil damp but not soggy, and prevent drying out at all times. Small seedlings

Make Furrows

Plant seeds

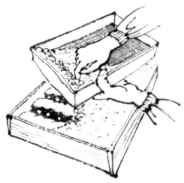

Cover with fine soil. Note sieve

Tamp down

should be watered with a fine spray or else merely dampen the soil, avoiding the plant itself. Keep a lookout for "damping off", which causes seedlings to rot at soil level and then to keel over. This is a fungal infection and may be controlled by a fungicide or by preliminary sterilisation of the soil. However, sterilisation is a troublesome procedure, and it is far more convenient to purchase a commercial potting mix. Another alternative is to use a mixture of pulverised peat moss and fine sand as a start-up medium.

When the seedlings are large enough to handle (usually with the appearance of the second leaf) carefully transplant them to small plastic pots 5–7 cm in diameter. When the young plants have fully established themselves, and are growing strongly, they may then be finally transferred to their permanent sites. When the time comes for the final transplantation, the pot can be squeezed gently and the whole root ball can be delivered intact. This manoeuvre is made easier if the soil is kept fairly dry.

An alternative is to start the seeds directly in these small pots. This is especially true for medium-sized seeds, such as tomato, cabbage, capsicum or lettuce. For example, with lettuce, sow four seeds in each pot, allow to germinate, then at a suitable time, thin out the seedlings to leave the strongest one to grow on. This eliminates the shock of the first transplantation. Correspondingly larger pots may be used for larger seed such as okra or squash. When the plant begins to outgrow the pot, knock out the rootball and plant into the ground or a larger container. Seeds may also be sown in peat pots. The whole pot with the growing seedling can be put in the ground at transplanting time. The peat pot disintegrates and allows roots to grow through into the surrounding soil. However, I have found that peat pots do not break up as readily as they are meant to do, thus hindering root growth. Besides, peat pots are fairly expensive.

Finally a word of warning about seeds. Seeds keep badly in our Hong Kong summers and so leftover seeds from the previous year should be discarded. Seed failure wastes precious time and effort, so always buy the best and freshest seed you can get, irrespective of price. Note that the expiry date printed on the seed package may not be a guarantee of viability. Seeds stored in excessive heat and humidity may have died off long before the sell-by date. There is no doubt that the initial outlay for a packet of good seed is the best investment a gardener can make. Any seed that you collect yourself should be properly dried, kept in sealed containers, and stored in a refrigerator.

Cuttings

This is the simplest and most popular method of vegetative propagation.

Softwood cuttings are taken from immature growing shoots and should be removed during the active growing period of the plant. Coleus and pelargonium are examples of plants suitable for this method. Semi-hardwood cuttings are taken from semi-mature wood and are usually employed to start shrubs, for example, hibiscus, bush clockvine and yellow jasmine. These are usually taken in spring or summer. Hardwood cuttings come from the mature wood and are taken during the dormant season. Semi-hardwood and hard

Softwood cutting

Semi-hardwood cutting

wood cuttings work best if they are "heel"' cuttings, that is, a cutting with a sliver or "heel" of bark from the donor stem still attached.

Softwood and semi-hardwood cuttings are usually rooted in an equal mixture of sand and peat moss. Sand taken from beaches may be used but only after a very thorough washing with fresh water to leach out the salt. However, most cuttings can root easily in ordinary garden soil provided that drainage is good. For convenience and good results, I now prefer to start cuttings in commercially available pre-packed potting soil or substrate.

Leaf cuttings are used for plants with thick fleshy leaves such as begonia and African violet. Depending on the individual plant, the whole leaf or part of it may be used for the cutting. In fact, many parts of the plant may be used for cuttings in addition to stems and leaves. Root cuttings, leaf bud cuttings and eye cuttings are examples. In laboratories plants can even be ground down and new plants raised from the mush or from tiny samples of DNA.

Leaf cutting

Leafbud cutting

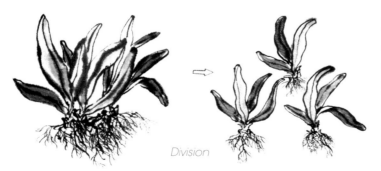

Division

Division

This is a quick way to propagate many perennials. The whole plant is lifted out of the soil and split into two or more clumps using a trowel, spade or other suitable instruments. Each clump can then be grown on as a new plant. Bamboo is an example of a plant that should be propagated in this way.

Layering

In this method of propagation, a stem or shoot of the parent plant is induced to produce roots while still attached to the parent. These shoots can later be detached to form independent plants.

Ground layering is used in plants with pendulous branches or those that have a trailing habit. The low branches are nicked with a sharp knife and then pegged down to just below soil level. Roots eventually appear from the wound and when the young plant is growing well it can be detached to grow on independently. Plants with runners, such as strawberry or spider plant, provide an easy and natural form of ground layering. The young plantlets at the end of the runners are simply pegged down to the soil or to satellite pots, to be detached when firmly rooted.

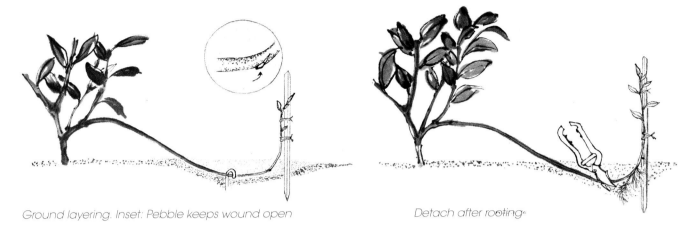

Ground layering. Inset: Pebble keeps wound open   *Detach after rooting.*

Air Layering

This is a more adventurous and interesting procedure. It is used for shrubs and trees where the branches cannot be brought down to ground level. Select a healthy growing branch which is suitable to form the main stem of the new plant. Create a wound on the branch by slitting it obliquely with a sharp knife. Alternatively, "ring" the bark, that is, scrape away the outer bark to expose the bare wood for about 5 cm. Pack the area around the wound with a damp rooting medium of mixed peat moss and garden soil. Enclose the whole by tying in a polythene sleeve at both ends, keeping the system airtight to prevent drying out. Roots will form from the wound and will be visible through the polythene. When the roots begin to pack the polythene sleeve, the branch can be detached and potted. This method may appear complicated to the beginner, but it is an interesting exercise and well worth trying for the experience. For a first attempt, try it with an azalea bush or with a rubber plant.

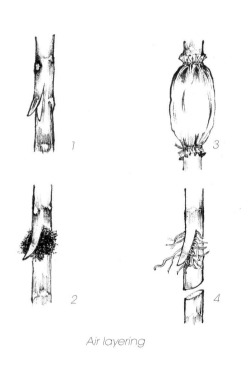

Air layering

Budding and Grafting

These are fairly complicated methods of propagation generally beyond the scope of the home gardener in Hong Kong. They are used for plants that do not come true from seed or that are difficult to raise by other methods. Most commonly, this applies to some roses and to some fruit and ornamental trees such as the flowering peach. For more information the reader should refer to a more complete garden manual.

Watering

One of the commonest questions asked by beginners is: "How often do I water it?" There is no simple answer to this question. To say that a plant should be given "enough" would be correct, but the advice would not be practical as different plants have different requirements. However, certain general rules apply. Firstly, watering must be thorough. Light watering means the water only penetrates the surface, leaving deeper roots still dry. It is better to water thoroughly and occasionally than lightly and often. The amount of watering also depends upon the drainage of the soil, this having been considered in an earlier section on soil. Always keep the soil properly loose and cultivated so that water can penetrate and will not simply run off the surface. For potted plants, watering must be particularly careful as conditions are likely to change more rapidly than with ground-grown plants. Do not be a slave to schedule: inspect, feel the soil, before deciding whether or not to water. Some shade-loving plants do better with overhead watering, helping the leaves to keep cool and free of dust. Sprinkling also discourages some pests such as spider mites. However, overhead watering may also promote disease such as mildew, especially when conditions are humid. Sprinkling can also damage delicate foliage and stems. When in doubt, avoid overhead watering.

Fertilising

The three most important nutrients for plants are nitrogen, phosphorus and potassium (Kalium), or "NPK". They are continuously used up by growing plants and must be replaced from time to time through fertilising.

Chemical fertilisers are convenient, and these mostly come in the form of a "complete" fertiliser, i.e., containing all the three essential nutrients. Naturally the actual content of the elements varies in different fertilisers and you will come across many fertilisers designed for special purposes—rose food, tomato food, lawn food and so forth. These specialist fertilisers are generally much more expensive and their claims sometimes extravagant. However, the cost is not that much for the home gardener and it is fun trying them out. Some plants, like camellia and rhododendron, thrive on acid plant foods and these special fertilisers are particularly useful in this group of plants. The actual percentage of nitrogen, phosphorus and potassium in any fertiliser is marked down in the packaging by numbers, for example 10–8–6. This means that the particular fertiliser contains 10% nitrogen, 8% phosphoric acid and 6% water-soluble potash.

Chemical fertilisers may come in solid or liquid form. Solid fertiliser in powder or pellet form is usually scattered on the soil surface or dug into the ground. They are useful in preparing the ground prior to planting. However, as they are in concentrated form, care must be used to avoid direct contact with the plant, otherwise "burning" will result. Some are meant to be dissolved in water before use. Foliar feeding refers to spraying a dilute liquid fertiliser to be directly absorbed by the leaves. A slow-release type of fertiliser spreads the feeding over a longer period of time, and in this way it presents a gentler way of feeding.

Organic fertilisers are derived from animal or vegetable sources. Examples are bone meal, peanut cake, fish oil, manure and so forth. Urine, diluted 1:10 is an excellent fertiliser for Chinese vegetables. Organic fertilisers are less strong than chemical fertilisers and therefore are less likely to cause "burning". This makes them safer to use, especially when transplanting.

Manure is the classic organic fertiliser. It is a complete fertiliser but one that is weak when judged by its NPK ratio. This is likely to be something like 1–1–1. Also, it is of little practical use to the home gardener because it is difficult to obtain, unpleasant to use, and often grows weeds. However, processed manure in pellet form is now quite easily available and is odourless until it is wet—and then it is not overly unpleasant. In the processing, the NPK value is much increased. Peanut cake (花生腐) is very popular and is certainly well rated by local farmers and gardeners. The "cake" is the solid residue left after the oil has been pressed out of the peanuts. It is an excellent and cheap all-round fertiliser and I can strongly recommend it. But it is also very popular with ants which may suddenly appear from nowhere in enormous numbers once peanut cake is laid down. The cake should therefore be properly covered with soil.

Most annual vegetables and flowers should be given a starter fertiliser at planting time. When the plant is established, another feed should be given. For anything else, feed when there is a noticeable growth spurt in the plant.

At this point it would be appropriate to mention compost, mulch and peat moss (or moss peat).

Compost

I have always been a great enthusiast of compost. Compost is made from waste vegetable matter which is allowed to break down to form a valuable source of humus and nutrients. It is a biological process of decomposition of organic material. Bacteria are the primary decomposing organisms, with assistance from worms, beetles, centipedes, maggots and fungi.

Those who do have sufficient space are strongly advised to set up a compost heap. Besides providing a ready source of an important soil conditioner, it gives one a great sense of satisfaction to be recycling waste: returning goodness taken from the soil back to the soil. From a practical standpoint, it is also a convenient way for the disposal of large amounts of garden waste. It is really amazing what huge volumes of garden waste can be swallowed up by a compost heap!

A ready-made compost bin is the simplest way to start. These bins are made of heavy plastic material and are neat and convenient to use. Garden waste is fed in from the top end and, after a few months, compost can be extracted from the lower end. Unfortunately I have not seen any on sale locally. They are easily available in garden centres overseas, and since they are usually of knock-down construction and not unduly bulky, it would be a simple matter to bring one back from your next trip abroad. However, a home-made compost heap is just as effective and easy to construct. Make a circular enclosure of heavy chicken wire. This should be about 1 m high and 1.5 m in diameter. The heap can also be made against a wall and should occupy some obscure and otherwise unused corner of the garden. Toss into the heap any manner of vegetable waste including such items as coffee grounds, sawdust, wood ash, tea leaves, potato peelings and even old newspapers. Avoid, however, material that decomposes slowly such as wood and stringy stalks. The compost bin is not a rubbish bin: food scraps, rags and kitty litter must not go in. The addition of lime will hasten the process of decomposition.

While it is maturing there are two requirements, namely air and moisture. Using chicken wire for the enclosure allows good circulation of air. A good compost heap generates a considerable amount of heat which indicates that the breakdown processes are in progress. The

Use chicken wire to enclose compost heap

heap needs to be aerated from time to time by turning the contents over with a pitch-fork. Water, as required, to keep the heap always moist. On the other hand, if the heap is too wet, add dry leaves or strips of newspaper. The compost should be ready for use in about four months, but before setting it out, first sift it through coarse-mesh chicken wire in order to remove undecomposed material, stones and so forth. When the compost is mature, it should be dark brown, odourless, crumbly and even-textured. It will then be ready for sprinkling on the lawn, as a top dressing for pot plants, or to be applied freely anywhere in the garden. Compost improves the physical nature of the soil which is so important for good growth and disease prevention. Because compost contains so many elements in the proper amount, it prevents the deficiency diseases such as dieback. With a good dose of well-made compost, many problems are alleviated or prevented.

Turning a compost heap

Mulch

Mulch is any material which is spread on the surface of the soil so as to reduce the loss of water by evaporation. It also helps to cool the surface in the hot summer sun, and to curtail the growth of weeds. Grass clippings, dead leaves, pine needles, tree bark, sawdust, peanut husks, half-rotted compost are examples of what can be used as mulch. Even small stones such as beach pebbles can be used for this purpose, especially for pot plants.

Peat Moss

Peat moss is a thick organic soil deposit with a low mineral content, derived largely from sphagnum moss and the roots of sedges and allied plants. It is flammable and burns with a characteristically sweet smell. It can be regarded as a very primitive form of lignite, which is a low-grade coal. Peat moss is ideal humus in a readily available form. When worked into the soil, it breaks down, supplying humus to condition a poor soil. It is essential to have some around any garden, but peat moss is little used by traditional Chinese gardeners. Peat moss is obtainable in small packets or 50 kg bags. It is convenient, clean and, most important, effective. Note, though, that peat moss has no intrinsic nutritive value. It is used for conditioning the soil, lightening heavy clay soils or improving the water retention capacity of a sandy soil. Dig it into beds, mix it with potting soil, or work it into the surface around growing plants. Being acid, it improves an alkaline soil and encourages acid-loving plants such as azaleas. Mixed with an equal part of sand, it is the standard rooting medium for cuttings. Of late, however, the use of peat moss has been declining rapidly as it has been rightly deemed environmentally unfriendly. Stocks of natural peat have been rapidly depleted, damaging flora and fauna and creating wasteland in many parts of the world. As a result, there is an appropriate upsurge of interest in compost, which in contrast to peat moss, is as wonderfully environmentally friendly as can be.

Pruning

The fundamentals of pruning must be understood in order to improve the quality of plants.

The total growth energy of a plant is directed to and shared by all its growing points. If any growing tip is removed, its share of growth energy will be redistributed to the remaining growing tips. If all the active growing tips are removed, then the remaining and otherwise dormant buds will receive a wake-up call, and will now have the means to burst forth into active growth. Having learned this lesson, you can now control a plant's growth behaviour and make it do the things you want. To make a plant bushier, remove one or more of the leading shoots to encourage side growth. For young, soft-stemmed plants such as coleus, this is done by the simple technique of "pinching out", that is, simply nipping off the tips between forefinger and thumb. If the aim is to produce one dominant stem or trunk, then the removal of all superfluous side shoots will

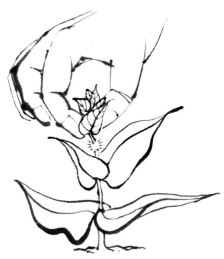

Pinching out

Pruning to produce a dominant stem   *Pruning for width*

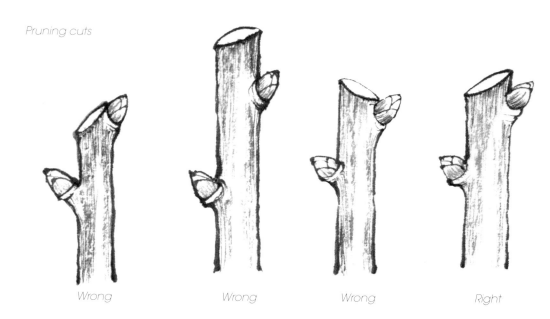

Pruning cuts

Wrong   *Wrong*   *Wrong*   *Right*

channel the growth potential to the chosen leader. On the other hand, if a shrub or tree is too tall and slender, rubbing off the leading shoot will force growth in width.

So far we have discussed pruning for shaping. Equally important is pruning for revitalising a weak plant. Removal of weak branches leads to new, stronger growth. Many shrubs and trees flower and fruit efficiently only on new growth. A flowering peach, for example, will bear flowers further and further out on long, willowy branches if left to itself year after year. Annual pruning keeps the tree compact, the flowers grouped together.

When pruning, make a clean cut above a bud—far away enough to avoid damaging it, but close enough to avoid leaving a stub. A stub is a dead end, and will "die back" to the bud, leaving it vulnerable to insects and decay. The bud chosen to be the new growing point should lead towards open space, in the direction you would like new growth to follow. Do not allow new branches to cross or to come into contact with one another. Always use a pair of sharp secateurs or scissors to make the cut.

Pests

Damage from pests can destroy a lot of hard work in a very short time. It often seems that pests strike just as your plants are reaching their peak. It is important, therefore, to be vigilant and to recognise any problems promptly. This is just another aspect of good garden practice.

There are many villains in the garden. Because they must first be identified, some of the more common offenders will be described and illustrated.

Caterpillars

Caterpillars are the larvae of moths and butterflies. They vary greatly in size and appearance. Some are hairy, others, smooth. They devour leaves very rapidly, leaving holes and notched edges. Remember though, that there are no butterflies without caterpillars. And what is a garden without butterflies?

Snails and Slugs

These are two of the most destructive pests in any garden. They feed at night in cool, wet conditions. Look for them among piles of dead vegetation. Slugs often inhabit the undersides of flower pots. They are frustrating adversaries because they disappear during the day and are not to be found anywhere. However, they leave a tell-tale trail of slime marks, thus betraying their movements and their location.

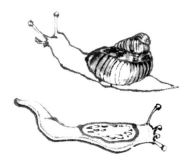

Aphids

These are small, green, black or yellow lice-like creatures. Some have wings, most look juicy. They are found in colonies, in large numbers, mostly on the under surfaces of leaves.

Mealy Bugs

These small, white, fuzzy insects are very slow-moving and usually found mingled in what looks like wisps of cotton wool. They inhabit under-sides of leaves, stem joints or roots.

Scale

These tenacious small pests attach themselves like limpets to the under surfaces of leaves and stems. They are tough customers to dislodge because they are covered by a protective shell. Many secrete a substance that attracts ants, thus compounding the problem.

Spider Mites

Pinpoint in size, these pests inhabit the undersides of leaves, producing a spidery web in which they move about.

Spittle Bugs

These bugs are usually surrounded by a protective froth or spittle, like cotton wool.

Thrips

Fast-moving, sucking insects that feed on buds, foliage and fruit.

Leaf Miners

These are easily recognised by the tortuous tunnels that they burrow just under the surface of a leaf which then begins to curl up.

Ants

These need no description. They are often found in conjunction with other pests such as aphids, scale and mealy bugs. Their nests injure roots and some feed on stems and foliage.

Pest Control

Shelves of supermarkets and seed shops are filled with a huge selection of chemicals that deal with pests. However, the first thing to remember is that indiscriminate, blunderbuss spraying is not good practice. It is best to avoid chemicals as far as possible. In a small garden or verandah it is possible to keep a close watch on the daily activity of pests, and chemicals can sometimes be dispensed with completely.

Physical Control

Large pests such as caterpillars, snails and slugs can be picked off individually and destroyed whenever they are found. Caterpillars often betray their presence by their droppings whereas snails and slugs give themselves away by leaving a trail of slime. When snails or slugs are present in large numbers, lay down wooden boards or cabbage leaves in the vicinity. Overturning these the next day will reveal many of the offenders obligingly attached to the boards or leaves and ready for disposal.

Aphids may be hosed off with water. Direct the spray of water upwards towards the undersides of the leaves where the pests are found in greatest number. Soapy water will often succeed where plain water has failed, either for aphids or mealy bugs.

Physical barriers to pests may be used in the form of nets to keep off sucking insects such as wasps, and fruit may be protected by paper bags. Flying insects may be trapped by deploying sticky traps.

Biological Control

Remember that ladybugs are natural enemies of aphids, consuming them in large numbers. Ladybugs are our great friends and should never be destroyed. Unfortunately there is nowhere in Hong Kong where ladybugs are available for sale. Some degree of biological control is afforded by inter-planting with repellent plants. For example, marigolds are known to be repellent to certain insects and nematodes.

Organic Sprays

All manner of concoctions have been devised in the search for a spray that works. Sprays containing extracts of tobacco, onions, shallots, garlic, detergents, sulphur all have their adherents. An organic spray based on neem oil is commercially available and is effective against a wide range of pests. It has fungicidal properties as well. Neem oil comes from the neem tree (*Azadirachta indica*), a relative of the mahogany. More information on these sprays can be found under "Organic Gardening".

Chemical Control

When a chemical is deemed necessary, a safe all-round performer is malathion. Malathion is effective against beetles, caterpillars, earwigs, aphids, mealy bugs, spider mites, spittle bugs, thrips, leaf miners, ants and mosquitoes to boot. It is a non-persistent insecticide which means it degrades rapidly to safe derivatives. However, it is advisable not to eat fruit or vegetable for two days after spraying.

When snails and slugs are difficult to control, lay down pellets of metaldehyde. The pests feed on the pellets with fatal results.

Whenever chemicals are used in the garden, it is absolutely essential to read carefully and to follow all instructions on the label. Keep all chemicals in a safe place out of the reach of children and pets. Lock them away when not in use. Avoid keeping large supplies—buy only what you need. Avoid inhaling sprays. Use a mask, and do not spray on windy days when the drift of the spray cannot be controlled. Spraying when rain is expected is a wasted effort as the chemical will be washed away. Always wash your hands after using chemicals.

Other destructive creatures in the garden include birds, cats and dogs. Birds attack ripening fruit and vegetable seedlings while cats and dogs do their damage by digging in fresh earth. Nets and coverings of chicken wire offer the best protection. Cats and dogs may also be kept away from newly transplanted plants by placing stones or tiles to cover the exposed ground in between. This is less unsightly than nets or wire mesh. At the time of writing I have six cats and one large dog who provide me with my share of problems.

Finally a few words about prophylaxis. Remember, strong, healthy plants withstand trouble best of all. Keep the garden clean at all times, clear rotting vegetation, dead insects, spilt foodstuffs, deadwood and all rubbish in general. Practise crop rotation even in the smallest garden. Look for disease-resistant seeds. Many diseases and pests that remain in the soil can be thwarted by moving plants around. Lastly, prevent spread of infestation by promptly removing and destroying diseased plants or portions of plants.

Plant Disorders

Pests destroy a basically healthy plant. However, the plant itself may suffer a wide variety of disorders resulting from–

Environmental Problems

These may be from wind damage, excessive shade, air pollution, excessive heat. Heat is a particular problem for containers and roof gardens.

Soil Problems

If drainage is poor, add vermiculite, perlite, coarse sand or polyurethane pellets to open up the spaces between the soil particles. Poor water retention is usually the result of a deficiency of organic matter. Treat this by adding peat moss or compost.

Nutritional Deficiencies

There may be a lack of one or more of the three most important elements, nitrogen, potassium and phosphorus. Test for this with simple soil kits. There may also be a lack of trace elements: boron, magnesium, manganese, molybdenum. Iron deficiency is quite common and presents with the condition known as "chlorosis". Chlorosis is easily recognised because the leaf begins to turn yellow while the veins remain a dark green. It can be readily treated by the addition of iron—a few tablets of iron sulphate (used to treat anaemia and available from any dispensary) will do very well.

Acid/Base Imbalance

Test the pH of the soil with simple metering equipment. Peat moss or sawdust will increase acidity; lime will increase alkalinity.

Plant Infections

These are serious intrinsic problems. Infection may be due to fungi, viruses or bacteria. Fungi cause problems such as mildew and can sometimes be tackled with commercial fungicides (usually compounds containing sulphur and copper). A viral infection is bad news and best dealt with by destroying the plants and disposing of them safely to prevent further spread.

Organic Gardening

I favour organic gardening but am not a slave to it. I almost exclusively use organic fertilisers. At present, my preference is for processed manure pellets, peanut cake, fish emulsion and, occasionally, bone meal. But I am not above using a foliar spray for ferns and such like. I make as much compost as possible—which is never enough— and use it freely. I avoid pesticides and use no weed killers at all. Large pests such as caterpillars, snails and slugs can be picked off by hand and many smaller pests such as aphids can be washed off with soapy water. Various slugs and snails can also be picked off, but I do resort to snail pellets occasionally.

There are many homemade concoctions that can be used as organic sprays. These are usually based on natural irritants such as tobacco, garlic, chilli and so on. Although not yet subjected to double-blind clinical trials, my current venom is soapy water in which some hot red chillies have been infusing. I am sure it is more effective than placebo! Remember though, to remove the chilli seeds which would otherwise foul up the spray mechanism. Even a whiff of this killer concoction is enough to bring tears to my eyes, and so—not a joke—protect your eyes when using this spray and never spray against the wind. It seems to work well enough initially, but it does lack some staying power. In my dim, dark laboratory, I am still working feverishly on the ultimate organic spray.

The protection of the environment extends even to small details, such as using bio-degradable coarse hemp twine for tying duties instead of wire twisties or plastic fasteners. This twine is easily and cheaply available from local hardware stores. Another example would be the use of bamboo canes for support rather than synthetic alternatives.

Whereas many organic gardeners swear by the superiority of their produce, this must still be considered a moot point. Many authorities would totally disagree. However, there is no doubt that the avoidance of pesticides is a healthy option and that eschewing strong chemicals is a boon to the planet.

A Note on Weeds

A weed is defined as a plant that tends to grow thickly where it is not wanted and which chokes out more desirable plants. I employ only one means of weed control—manual extirpation. I use no chemical weed killers whatever. Although a chore hated by most gardeners, I must confess I find weeding relaxing and strangely therapeutic. It is particularly effective if I am upset, or when all the world seems to be at odds with me. Peace of mind returns, and troublesome thoughts vanish as I sit on my little stool, winkling out the clearweed, crabgrass, plantain and whatnot. There is also a great deal of satisfaction to be gained from having cleared an unruly patch of ground, and enjoying the result.

Some weeds are distinctly attractive, such as pennywort, ageratum, artillery clearweed, spurge and others. I feel almost apologetic about destroying them and sometimes leave them alone if they are doing no harm. A weed, after all, has been alternatively defined as a plant whose virtues have not yet been recognised. I further let the side down by encouraging se-lected weeds, such as wild ferns and wild Chinese spinach (for the table). Some weeds, though, resent my intervention and retaliate vigorously: sorrel by exploding its seed capsules upon the slightest touch, bombarding me with its missiles (it could have been the inspiration for the cluster bomb) while its kin, lavender sorrel, perversely and wilfully causes its compound rhizome to disintegrate and fall through your fingers just when you think you have dug it out whole. If only there were a way to measure the IQ of plants!

On a more serious note, weeding is a necessary chore around the garden, and must never be put off for too long. It is, after all, part of good housekeeping. Some of the more aggressive weeds must be given no quarter, and must be wiped out on sight. Prominent among these is *Mikania micrantha*, otherwise known as "mile-a-minute weed". It is a tropical American vine that was once introduced to India during World War II to camouflage airfields. It has now taken to camouflaging everything in sight, all around the world. It is rampant in the Hong Kong countryside and in any piece of urban wasteland. Thankfully, it is less likely to be a problem in a small garden, and not a problem at all in verandahs and patio gardens—but you never can tell, so look out for a twining weed with dark green cordate leaves that travels quickly.

Weeds succeed because they have mastered the Darwinian principle of survival of the fittest. Therefore, they are more likely to proliferate than whatever you have planted in the ground. They also have their own requirements of space, light, water and nutrients which must be shared among themselves and your desirable plants. Early elimination is thus of paramount importance. Also, a certain amount of discipline is crucial as this task needs to be carried out on a regular basis. Invest in a good quality narrow hand fork, and look for any special tools that will make weeding easier. A long, sturdy screwdriver is wonderful for awkward spaces and deep roots.

Plant Taxonomy: How Plants Are Named

Before we deal with individual plants, we should first consider how plants receive their names. Taxonomy is the science of classification. In plant taxonomy, the taxa are, in descending order—kingdom, phylum, class, order, family, genus and species. For practical purposes, we will confine ourselves to the last three.

A plant's name is written in the official scientific language, Latin, and begins with its **genus,** much like a surname. Within the genus are a number of individual **species,** the name of which is written after the genus name. Therefore, *Aesculus pavia* belongs to the genus *Aesculus* and the species *pavia.* Note that they are written in italics with the first letter of the genus name in upper case and the first letter of the species name in lower case. The species name also gives some indication of the plant's characteristics. For example, *semperflorens* (always flowering), *fragrans* (fragrant), *sinensis* (from China), *pumila* (dwarf), *spectabilis* (showy), and so forth. Most plants are thus known by this combination of two names, genus and species. This combination, or binomial, was the idea of the Swedish naturalist Carolus Linnaeus (1707–1778).

A collection of several related genera make up a **family.**

Growing in the wild or in the garden, a species may, over time, develop some differences in colour or form while retaining the general characteristics of the species. These modified forms are known as **varieties.** The variety name follows the species name, such as *Aesculus pavia humilis,* and is also written in italics with its first letter in lower case.

Some new forms which arise not in the wild, but as a result of deliberate manipulation during cultivation, are known as **cultivars.** The name of the cultivar is written in ordinary type within single quotation marks as in *Aesculus hippocastinum* 'Baumannii'. The cultivar sometimes bears the name of its creator, and the first letter is in upper case.

Crossing two species belonging to the same genus results in a **hybrid,** which exhibits some properties of both species. A hybrid is usually created to produce novel forms, an improved appearance, better growth habits, or improved resistance to diseases and pests. A hybrid is given a Latin name prefixed by an "x" sign, as in *Aesculus x carnea.* A **F1** hybrid is a first generation cross between two pure strains. An **F2** hybrid is a second generation cross between two F1 hybrids.

It is also possible to cross two different but related genera, in which case the "x" sign precedes the name as in x *Cupressocyparis.* It is a hybrid between the genera *Cuppressus* and *Chamaecyparis.*

Considering there are about 300,000 species of flowering plants, conifers, cycads, ferns and allies in existence, the development of this relatively simple system by which they can be clearly identified and classified is a genuine triumph of human endeavour.

Common names follow no hard and fast rules. They are usually descriptive of the form and colour of the plant, or its resemblance to everyday objects, for example, "red powder puff" or "purple heart". Other names are dreamily poetical as in "Song of India". A plant's dazzling beauty may warrant an extravagant name such as "Queen of the night". Melodrama is also an influence such as in "love-lies-bleeding". Some, of course, are named for no reason at all, as in "periwinkle". Using common names may lead to some confusion as many plants have more than one common name and may be known by still other names in different languages and dialects.

Gardening Hints for Hong Kong

Gardening Hints for Hong Kong

Weather

For gardeners everywhere, weather is a major consideration. Hong Kong lies just within the tropics, at latitude 22°N and longitude 114°E, and has four distinct seasons. The absence of a really cold winter means that we can enjoy 365 growing days a year. The coldest winter day in urban areas seldom sees temperatures of below 5°C though lower temperatures do occur in the open ground of the northern New Territories and on high ground. Having said that, it is good to remember that certain plants described as "hardy" are, in fact, hardy only down to about 6°C, so cold damage can and does occur from time to time. Some plants are even more delicate and may sustain damage when the temperature falls below 13°C. But a change seems to have come upon us, even in a relatively short span of twenty years—probably the result of the abuse of the environment on a global scale. We can see the later onset of winter, which also now tends to be warmer. Seeds that once could be sown on the first of September would, for best results, now be sown upon a noticeable fall in the temperature, usually mid-September or even October.

The biggest single weather problem is the typhoon and its younger sibling, the tropical storm. In an average year we can expect three or more such events between June and October. Violent winds and torrential rains wreak havoc in the garden.

The main defence against the typhoon is withdrawal. Since the local gardener is likely to do a lot of planting in containers, it means considerable damage can be averted if anything movable is removed indoors or to some form of shelter. Stow away loose objects such as buckets and brooms, and batten down whatever else that is not practical to move. Top heavy potted plants (such as palms), that need to remain outdoors should be laid sideways down on the ground in anticipation of their being blown down. Many valuable containers may be smashed otherwise.

Flooding should be prevented by ensuring all drains are clear and working. Flooding often causes more damage to young plants than wind and rain combined.

If a particularly bad typhoon is threatening, it is a worthwhile effort to thin out large-leaved plants and to trim dense foliage from trees. Some trees that are easily snapped by gusts of wind, such as papaya and cassia, should be roped securely. There is now nothing left to do except to wait out the storm and then to pick up the pieces. Do not forget to trim away storm-damaged portions of plants and trees.

Quite apart from typhoons, heavy rain showers between May and September can bring much trouble especially to seedlings. This is why you will be well advised to sow seeds in pans or pots whenever possible, even for some of those varieties that normally prefer to be sown in the ground and left undisturbed. The defence strategy of withdrawal can then be applied to these pans and pots. If you insist on sowing autumn annuals in the ground, wait till mid-October when the danger of rains will have subsided.

Hong Kong sees a seasonal reversal of wind direction and can, therefore, be said to have a monsoon climate. The prevailing winds throughout the year, however, are the easterlies. The winter monsoon begins around the end of September to mid-March, blowing from the northeast and bringing noticeably cooler and drier conditions. The onset of the winter monsoon is the traditional signal for farmers to plant winter vegetables. Similarly, it informs the home gardener that he should plant his autumn sown annuals. This planting can go on in succession until November or early December. Autumn is thus to the Hong Kong gardener what spring is to his counterparts in temperate climates. It is, in fact, the busiest period of the gardening year. Be warned though, that the winter monsoons are often very strong; and being very dry as well, they can destroy young seedlings overnight unless protection and adequate water are provided. Do not forget the importance of mulching at this time.

The onset of spring brings coastal mist and fog when the warm, humid south-easterly maritime winds meet with the cold north-easterlies. Spring planting usually takes place around the middle of March. However, if by this time the weather has not yet warmed up or if it is still damp and windy, delay planting until the conditions improve. In fact, many local farmers will not start their warm weather vegetables like string beans and Chinese spinach until after the traditional Ching Ming festival.

Space Saving Suggestions

In a place like Hong Kong a few words on space efficiency will surely help you make full use of your available space. Here are a few suggestions:

Plant More Densely

Many plants, especially vegetables, will grow in much less space than you may think. In later sections of this book you will find further advice with individual plants. For example, a well known gardening text advises that kohlrabi should be grown in rows 35 cm apart, thinning the seedlings to 15 cm apart. In fact, kohlrabi will grow very well 15 cm apart each way—you can easily grow two rows in the space suggested for one. Growing vegetables in clumps with all plants equidistant is certainly more efficient than in rows, especially when only a small number of plants is needed. However, planting more densely also means more attention must be paid to the individual plant, such as removing withered leaves to let in more light, clearing weeds more frequently, and carefully cultivating the soil to keep it loose and in good condition. I am sure we are all more than willing to lavish a little more attention on our plants if this means we can produce more.

Start Seeds in Pans

Some seeds are best sown directly in the ground where they are to grow. While this may be the ideal method for some plants, one can bend the rules a little and start the seeds in pans or pots. In this way seedlings can be raised even before ground is available, so no time is lost. When space does become available, the established young plant will be ready to occupy it. Once again, more individual attention for the seedlings is necessary in order to overcome or at least minimise the trauma of transplantation which would not have been necessary if seeds were sown in the ground. Some advice on this matter is given in the section on "Basic Gardening".

Use Containers

The use of containers is a great space-saving method. Prime garden space can be fully utilised by switching pots around as plants reach and pass their prime. Meanwhile, new plants can be grown in less conspicuous areas such as roof-tops, backyards and so on. See "Containers".

Use Vertical Space

Floor area is not the only available space in a garden. Walls, fences, gates—all these can be utilised. Small pots hanging randomly on a gate or a wall add a totally new dimension. Exploit all possibilities for climbing plants, which be-sides providing colour can be used as screens or as cover-ups for ugly areas like drainpipes.

The Concrete Garden

Gardening without a garden? Why not? Just look up at any high-rise and you will see veran-dahs spilling over with greenery, pots jostling for space with the day's laundry and other evidence of valiant attempts at growing things. In our crowded city, urban gardeners work on verandahs, rooftops, postage stamp gardens, and even sampans. Not ideal, perhaps, but not as restrictive as you may think!

Gardening on verandahs, patios and rooftops poses special problems. Most plants would need to be grown in pots or containers. Those of us who have rooftops, patios or backyards may also build permanent beds along the perimeter walls. What can be grown in a relatively shallow bed is truly astonishing. In soil half a metre deep, small trees and shrubs can thrive—papaya, peach, azalea and many others as well. Grass grows in 7 cm of soil.

Building a bed is no haphazard matter, the problems being proportional to the size. The first consideration if you are a rooftop gardener is to make sure your roof is truly waterproof. Should there be any doubts, lay down a fresh layer of concrete or, if necessary, seek professional advice from a builder.

Examine the available drains and do not build over them. Determine the slope of the floor by observing the direction of drainage after hosing down with water. The retaining wall should be of solid construction, say brick, and if the top is wide enough the wall may provide additional casual seating. Drainage holes should be made at intervals. If the bed is a large one, drainage water may spread over the whole floor and keep it unpleasantly wet. If so, build a low drainage gutter along the foot of the bed to lead the water to the drains. It goes without saying that large beds must not be built in the middle of any roof unless it has adequate structural support underneath.

One consistent problem with roof gardens is heat. Strong sun beating down on a tiled or concrete surface generates heat that hurts to the touch. Imagine what it can do to your plants. Plants already confined within containers are liable to be literally cooked to death unless provided with suitable shade. Raising the pot a few inches off the ground with "feet" of brick or tiles also helps. Adequate watering is also a priority.

I must also say something about a lawn. Nothing gives a garden a sense of space more than a lawn, and rooftop or backyard gardeners need not be deprived of this pleasure. It sounds ridiculous, but an attractive lawn can be grown, as mentioned above, in no more than 7 cm of soil. So, include a patch of grass, however tiny, in your plans.

My own garden is largely a concrete-surfaced backyard which supports, among other things, a 100-m² lawn—much to the disbelief of many visitors. Pay particular attention to providing good drainage, as I learned the hard way after the first rainstorm. Whatever you do, please do not use artificial grass!

Careful planning can result in an amazing transformation of a sterile slope to a garden setting. A few years ago, a crumbling shotcrete slope beneath my verandah was in dire need of repair. The estate managers were about to simply renew the shotcrete when I intervened and tried to convince them to let me fill the lower bit with soil and plant a garden. My neighbours made grumbling noises about cost and maintenance, but fortunately, I prevailed. With plants from my own garden and from friends, the 30 m long planter, which I now refer to as my "Accidental Garden", was put together at negligible cost—if you factor out the backache. The result can be seen in the front and back inside covers.

Containers

To some people a container means a clay pot. In fact, containers come in any shape and size. Urns, cooking pots, wooden crates, baskets, tubs … the list is endless, and new ideas about containers keep cropping up all the time to an innovative gardener. In Hong Kong we have a particularly varied choice of interesting containers. Flowerpots range from a humble unglazed clay pot to a finely decorated artistic porcelain for which the Chinese are justly famous. The most useful large container for general use is the "dragon" urn in which preserved duck eggs were once shipped. These are highly decorative, durable and reasonably priced. Of course, nowadays, eggs are no longer packed in these urns. Instead, these urns are specifically made as containers for plants. The large variety of earthenware cooking utensils also provides an interesting range of shapes and sizes from which to choose. Chinese wine, preserved vegetables and various kitchen ingredients also come in some fascinating containers. Naturally, in all of these, drainage must be provided by chipping a hole in the bottom with the careful use of a stout nail and hammer.

In recent years plastic pots have become very popular. These are cheap with other advantages such as being easily stacked for storage, easily cleaned, and above all, light. Shifting heavy pots is one of the more damaging forces on your lower back. Smaller plastic pots are very useful for raising young plants prior to final transplantation. With a gentle squeeze and a tap on the bottom, the whole contents can be delivered intact with minimal disturbance to the root ball. Egg trays, fruit trays, plastic drinking cups and plastic bags may also be used in similar fashion, but the small plastic pots, so cheap and convenient, have supplanted these in my own practice.

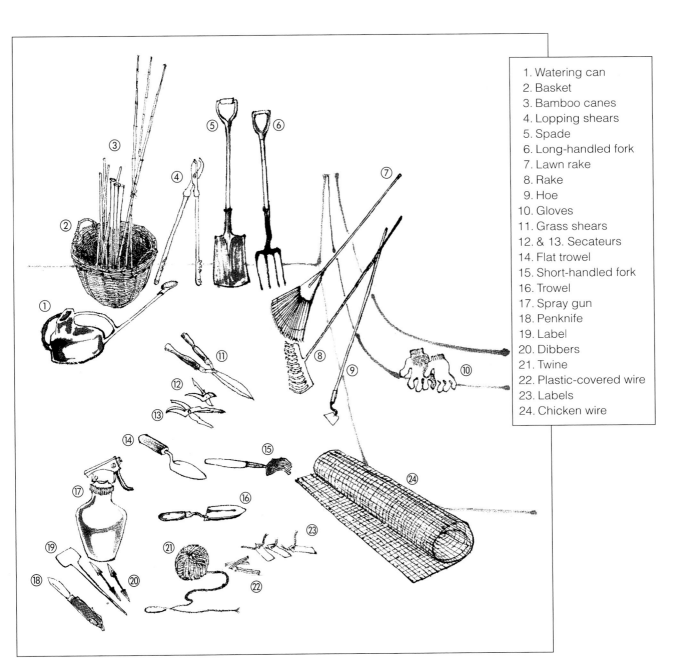

1. Watering can
2. Basket
3. Bamboo canes
4. Lopping shears
5. Spade
6. Long-handled fork
7. Lawn rake
8. Rake
9. Hoe
10. Gloves
11. Grass shears
12. & 13. Secateurs
14. Flat trowel
15. Short-handled fork
16. Trowel
17. Spray gun
18. Penknife
19. Label
20. Dibbers
21. Twine
22. Plastic-covered wire
23. Labels
24. Chicken wire

For indoor display, planters add a touch of sophistication to pot plants. Brought indoors and placed in a decorative planter, an otherwise dull plant may be transformed, Cinderella-like, into an exciting display. Try using some of the endless variety of basket ware so easily obtainable in Hong Kong. Like containers, planters come in any shape, form and material—it is up to you to make the best of what is available.

Container plants need special care. Always start out with a clean pot. Any old soil, adherent roots and assorted detritus must be scrubbed away and the pot thoroughly washed. This helps to eliminate any disease or pests that may have affected the previous plants. Next, provide adequate drainage. Having made sure the drainage hole is adequate, cover it with a curved shard or a square of fine wire mesh. If especially good drainage is required, spread a layer of gravel, coarse sand, granulated charcoal, or polyurethane pellets that you find in packing cases (for electrical goods, for example) on the bottom. The polyurethane pellets have the advantage of being light, making any moving of the containers a less heavy task.

While drainage is important, also remember that pot plants dry out much more readily than ground-grown plants. Mulching with small stones is particularly useful for containers, as other forms of mulch tend to be washed away by watering. Another helpful trick is to use metal foil discs normally employed for protecting kitchen gas rings. These are circles of foil with a central opening for the gas ring. Cut open the foil at one point with a radial scissor-cut and slip the disc around the base of the plant. Weigh the disc down with a few stones and you now have an effective, long-lasting "mulch".

Plants that outgrow their pots must be potted-on. This occurs when the root system becomes packed and starts to grow out of the drainage hole or spills over the surface. Having removed the plant from its old container, shake off as much old soil as possible. With a sharp knife shave the edges of the root ball and score the roots lightly, loosening them as you do so. This helps to stimulate new growth of roots. Now place the plant in the next size of container and fill the empty space around it with fresh earth and mix in some slow-release fertiliser or manure pellets. The best time for re-potting is during the plant's dormant season before the spurt of new growth.

For plants grown in large containers, it is of course not practical to re-pot. If the growth of, say, a pot-grown shrub appears to be sluggish and the soil root-bound, try to revitalise it with root pruning. Use a long, flat, sharp instrument and work around the edges of the pot. Remove the root prunings, loosen the edge of the root ball and extract as much old soil as possible. The resulting space around the edges can now be filled with new earth or compost mixed with a non-burning feed such as slow-release fertiliser or manure pellets.

WESTERN MARKET

Where to Buy Supplies

I know of no gardening centre in Hong Kong where one may find a comprehensive stock of gardening requirements under one roof. Local nurseries are mostly quite unsophisticated despite vast improvements having taken place in recent years. From these nurseries one may obtain small trees, vines and other young plants and shrubs. Most would specialise in certain varieties of plants, especially potted plants.

The best source of seeds, especially vegetable seeds, is a cluster of shops on Hong Kong side just beyond Western Market 西港城 (Sheung Wan MTR station). These shops cater mainly to professional local gardeners and farmers, and stock an excellent variety of seeds, fertilisers, bulbs, sprays and other supplies including some tools. Many seeds may be bought loose, by the pinch or by the pound, often with some helpful over-the-counter advice as a bonus. To shop for plants, there is no better location than Flower Market Road 花墟道 in Mongkok (Prince Edward MTR station). Collected within two city blocks, you will find several dozen shops selling pot plants, cut flowers, gardening implements, containers and other paraphernalia. A few shops stock seeds as well.

Seeds may also be ordered from overseas suppliers by post, phone, fax or e-mail. Catalogues list a huge number of plants, but remember to choose carefully as not all are suited to Hong Kong conditions.

BEWARE OF DOG

Plants from
A to Z

African violet 非洲紫羅蘭
Saintpaulia

This is one of the most popular of all urban indoor plants, hardly requiring description. These plants were originally collected from their native North Africa by Baron von Saint Paul. There are 20 species of this low-growing perennial and several thousand varieties.

There are many people who "specialise" in African violets, as witness the unending range of soil mixes, fertilisers, pots, conditioners and what-have-you specially designed for them. They are best grown indoors, in open shade, away from the direct rays of the sun. They are particularly comfortable in offices since they thrive in fluorescent light. Also, because they like cool days and warm nights, an air-conditioned fluorescent-lit office is close to the ideal environment. Properly cared for, a plant will flower freely for most of the year.

Grow *Saintpaulia* in a light, well-drained soil mix comprising equal parts of loam, peat moss, sand and leaf mould. Alternatively, convenient ready-made mixes are commercially available. Keep the soil moist but never water-logged. Avoid the leaves when watering to prevent them from being marked. Feed once a week with a dilute liquid fertiliser.

Although it can be propagated from seed, it is more usual to use a leaf cutting. Remove a healthy leaf from a strong plant. Use a sharp razor blade, leaving about 4 cm of the leaf stalk attached to the leaf. Insert the cuttings singly in small pots containing equal parts of sand and peat moss. Keep the leaf off the soil to prevent rotting. Plantlets appear in four to six weeks and they should be potted-on as they outgrow their containers.

Alternatively, the cuttings can be rooted in water. Roots appear earlier by this method but the roots are very delicate and easily damaged. However, with careful handling there is no reason why new plants cannot be raised with equal success in this manner.

Ageratum 藿香薊
Ageratum houstonianum

An attractive dwarf species most suited to our gardens because of its compact growth. The dusty-blue flowers are collected into heads that resemble shaving brushes packed together. A white variety is also available. Seeds may be sown in spring or autumn. In the wild *Ageratum conyzoides* (勝紅薊) is a rampant weed, 30–60 cm high with flowers similar to the cultivated garden species but with a more open and spare growth. Nevertheless, a bank of these wild flowers can be very eye-catching. It flowers all year round.

Allamanda (trumpet vine) 軟枝黃蟬
Allamanda cathartica

This is a climbing shrub of South American origin, with very attractive, bright yellow, trumpet-shaped flowers 10 cm across. The flowers appear from March to November, providing continuous and abundant colour for many months. The dark green lance-shaped leaves are arranged in whorls and bleed a milky sap if cut. All parts of the plant are poisonous, resulting, as one would expect from the species name, in diarrhoea. Beautiful, reliable and trouble-free, it has my full recommendation. Properly pruned, it is also a handsome shrub, now very popular in public gardens.

Cuttings of 12 cm of the previous year's wood will root readily in a mixture of peat moss and sand. They are best taken in spring or summer. Pot-on the rooted cuttings as necessary. Allamanda is at its best when allowed to climb, but it requires considerable space and full sun. A vigorous performer, it is extremely useful for covering fences and walls or for masking ugly drain-pipes. Pinch out the leading shoots when the desired height is reached and train to the supports as required. Grown as a shrub, the shoots should be stopped when they reach a length of about 20 cm. This encourages side growth and a bushy habit. Allamanda may also be pot-grown, but as it has a vigorous root system, it requires potting-on annually.

In February, prune shrubs severely to within one or two nodes of the old wood. Climbers, too, require considerable cutting back.

Another variety, the **small allamanda** (硬枝黃蟬, *Allamanda nerifolia*) is a non-climbing shrub producing yellow tubular flowers 5 cm across. It is not as showy as the larger version, but because of its slower and bushier growth, it may be more suitable if space is limited.

Alocasia 海芋
Alocasia odora

Alocasia is a tropical Southeast Asian plant found in the wild state throughout Hong Kong. Its large heart-shaped, mid-green leaves grow from a short stem. The leaves are very decorative and resemble taro leaves, which is not surprising, since it is closely related to *Colocasia*. Local fruit sellers often display their wares on these leaves, taking advantage of their large size to provide a fresh green background. In a home setting, these large leaves may be used as table decoration or as place mats, especially for alfresco events. Its long-stemmed, arum-like flowers are not particularly attractive.

Although generally regarded as a weed, a young specimen makes an excellent house plant as it tolerates shade very well. When the plant outgrows its pot, discard it and replace it with a new one, which can be found on virtually any shady hillside in Hong Kong. In the garden, it is very suitable for a sunless corner.

The plant is also said to have medicinal properties against hypertension and other ailments. On the other hand, its sap contains poisonous crystals that can cause numbness and swelling of the tongue or a severe skin rash.

Angel's trumpet 洋金花 / 曼陀羅

Brugmansia syn. *Datura*

The tropical or subtropical *Brugmansia* and *Datura* are closely related. The taller, woody shrubs or small trees are now generally included under *Brugmansia*. True *Daturas* are short-lived herbaceous plants with smaller, more upright flowers. The shrub is rather irregular in shape and is grown for its spectacular, pendulous, trumpet-shaped white flowers. The long, fluted shafts are formed by five fused petals which are slightly wavy at the margins and which curve back voluptuously to a sharp point. The flowers open fully at night, releasing an intense fragrance with a hint of ginger, and partially close during the day. Flowering begins around December and continues into the summer. A site sheltered from strong winds is preferred as the branches snap easily. Good soil and at least four hours of sunshine a day are also needed. It can be very successfully grown in pots and in full flower it makes a striking display. At the end of the flowering period, it should be pruned hard to 15 cm from the ground. If a larger shrub is required, then it can simply be cut back by about a third. Propagate by cuttings taken any time in summer. I have only seen the white variety in Hong Kong, but there are cultivars with purple, yellow, and sometimes double flowers.

All parts of the plant are poisonous and have been used by primitive tribes as medicines, narcotics and poisons.

Arctotis (African daisy) 非洲菊

Arctotis sp.

Not to be confused with *Gerbera*, though the flowers are similar. It is not often seen in Hong Kong although it succeeds admirably. Arctotis is grown as an autumn-sown annual and is very suitable for pots or borders. Sow the seeds from September to November in pans. Prick out the seedlings into boxes for hardening before planting in an open, sunny site or in pots, two plants to a 12-cm pot. It grows very quickly producing attractive woolly, silvery green leaves. When the growing tip reaches 12 cm tall, pinch it out to encourage a bushy habit. The flowers are mostly orange-coloured with a black central disc. They tend to close in the evening and in dull weather. The blooms are short-lived but appear in quick succession. Dead-head to extend the flowering period.

Asclepias (blood flower, butterfly weed) 馬利筋 / 連生桂子花

Asclepias curassavica

This is a small shrub producing umbels of reddish-orange flowers followed by spindle-shaped seed pods about 5 cm long. It is easily raised from seed and indeed grows wild in some parts of Hong Kong. Flowers are produced all year long. Interesting rather than beautiful, I have grown it for a few seasons out of curiosity but must admit it is not one of my favourites.

Asparagus 露筍

Asparagus officinalis

The edible asparagus is seldom grown. It is a vegetable of antiquity, mentioned in writings before the time of Christ. A perennial, it is believed to originate from the Mediterranean region. It dies down in winter to re-emerge in the spring. The spears grow into tall stems, later becoming much branched, with a fern-like appearance somewhat similar to *Asparagus plumosus*. The delicate, feathery ferns are useful for flower arrangements. When the plant is well established after its spring resurrection, the spears can be harvested when they are about 10 cm long. It can be grown from seed but takes two to three years to produce worthwhile spears. Alternatively, grow from "crowns" which are obtainable from garden centres abroad, though not locally.

Asparagus spears

Asparagus (ornamental)

Asparagus sp.

Despite being known as ferns, they belong in fact, to the lily family in a broad sense. There are two plants that are commonly called the asparagus fern.

Asparagus plumosus (文竹) looks quite different from *A. sprengeri* (天冬). This is grown for its frond-like, feathery foliage. The stems are stiff with prickles and the fronds are thrown out horizontally to provide a layered appearance. Very popular as a pot plant, it is non-climbing when young. Mature plants, however, climb widely both by using their prickles and by twining around any support. Grown against an iron gate it can provide a delicate-looking screen. It is best grown in open shade. Propagate by division or from seed. Young plants are plentiful and cheap in garden shops or stalls.

A. sprengeri is a bushy perennial climber with small stiff leaves. It bears small white flowers which give rise to pea-sized berries, green at first, later turning a bright red. This plant is mostly grown as a pot plant and is especially suitable for hanging baskets as its long curving branches arch gracefully down to produce a soft trailing effect. It grows quite rapidly and should be potted-on as the roots crowd together. Divide the plants for propagation. It can also be raised from seed. If grown with some support nearby, it can climb, using small hooked prickles that cover its wiry stems. Growth slows down in the summer while new growth appears with the approach of cooler weather in September.

Asparagus sprengeri

Aster 翠菊

The **Chinese aster** (*Callistephus chinensis*) is a popular flower in the Chinese New Year flower markets. These asters are erect plants with solitary daisy-like flowers in red, pink, purple or white. The leaves are coarsely toothed. They are good cut flowers, though at the Chinese New Year markets the whole plant is sold, roots and all.

Plant in October and grow in full sun and well-drained soil. Some may require staking. Removal of the first dead flowers improves flowers carried on side shoots.

The aster known also as **Michaelmas daisy** (荷蘭菊) belongs to the genus *Aster*. The flowers are all daisy-like though in many different forms—frilled, pom-poms, etc. Most have yellow centres. Cultivation is the same as for Chinese aster.

Avocado 牛油果
Persea

The pear-shaped, crinkly-surfaced, dark-green avocado as found in supermarkets is imported from temperate regions of the world. Avocado trees are rare locally, but all those I have seen produce smooth-skinned fruit, either mid-green or brown. The fruit is also much larger, perhaps 300–400 g. This is the tropical form of avocado, probably originating from the Philippines or from the West Indies, and is most likely *Persea americana*.

The fruiting avocado is a large tree and can only be grown by the favoured few with large gardens. Even then it needs regular pruning to limit its size. I am fortunate to have one of these trees which I started from the stone of an avocado obtained from a friend's garden in Kowloon Tong. This marvellous garden, large, dark, fecund and largely neglected, was attached to a fine old house, dating from the early 1900s. It had in it two huge avocado trees, each 20 m high, producing hundreds of fruit each year, most of which went to waste. It takes seven to ten years from planting before fruit can be expected. My own tree, which I planted on a hillside next to my house, now keeps me in good supply every year from July to September.

The received wisdom concerning avocado is that a single tree will not bear fruit because it is incapable of self-fertilisation. Another nearby tree or group of trees is therefore said to be essential to fruiting. I can only say this: I have one avocado tree which I believe to be the only one in the neighbourhood, and I have never been short of avocados.

A small avocado tree makes an excellent, decorative pot plant, easily raised from seed. An avocado seed will germinate in a pot of ordinary soil with good drainage. It will even oblige if simply left standing in half a saucerful of water. Grow in good light and keep the plant bushy by well-planned pruning.

The avocado is second only to the olive in oil content among fruits. This is reflected in its Chinese name of "butter fruit". However, the fat in avocado is of the monounsaturated variety which is "healthy" fat. It raises the blood level of high-density "good" cholesterol while lowering low-density "bad" cholesterol.

Azalea 杜鵑

Rhododendron

A well-loved evergreen shrub producing masses of colourful flowers in spring. In recent years more and more planting of azaleas has resulted in it being seen just about everywhere in Hong Kong.

The **red azalea** (紅杜鵑, *Rhododendron simsii*) is actually a salmon pink colour. It is taller, more slender and smaller-leaved than the other common variety, the **purple azale**a (紫杜鵑, *R. pulchrum*). Flowers are very dense, eclipsing the rest of the bush. Pink and pure white varieties are also available. *R. pulchrum* is a stockier, bushier, leafier shrub, producing larger blooms in smaller numbers but provides an equally spectacular burst of colour as *R. simsii*. This variety is also successfully grown in pots. However, the larger the container the better. A dragon urn is most suitable and supports a large bush. It is still attractive out of flower, more so than the red variety. The **Japanese azalea** (日本杜鵑, *R. indicum*) has small 3-cm leaves and smaller flowers in pink, white, salmon or cerise.

Azaleas need a good deal of sun. However, reasonable shrubs can be grown in part shade. The azalea is the classic acid-loving plant and will not tolerate an alkaline soil. Many specialist fertilisers that supply the acid it requires are available. Acid can also be provided by frequent application of peat moss or sawdust. In terms of nitrogen requirement, azaleas do not need much feeding. However, they require a soil rich in humus which retains water yet allows excess water to drain away quickly. Azaleas are surface rooters and the soil should not be cultivated around them. Mulching is important. Generally no regular pruning is required. However, large plants can be cut back and growing tips can be pinched back to encourage bushier growth if required. This should be carried out after the flowering period. Propagation is by air layering. Those who have never tried this form of propagation will find it an interesting and rewarding experience with azaleas.

Bamboo 竹

Bambusa sp.

Bamboo is intricately woven into eastern lore. The hundred or so species vary considerably in form, and many play a role in some way in everyday life. In art, bamboo is featured in paintings, furniture and cultural artefacts. On a more practical note, bamboo has great importance in construction with its straight stems, light weight and immense structural strength. It is still the most popular scaffolding material in Hong Kong. Its quick growth provides a steady source of replaceable material, a quality more recently exploited in the making of paper.

In the small garden, a suitable bamboo for planting is the dwarf **Buddha bamboo** (佛肚竹, *Bambusa ventricosa*) which grows 1–3 m tall. The whole plant is bushy and very compact. The internodes are slightly swollen producing a decorative ringed effect, more especially if the roots are confined. It is suitable for a container such as an urn or a large tub. Young plants of **golden bamboo** (銀竹, *B. vulgaris*) may also be grown in large containers or planters. The feathery foliage of bamboo epitomises a restful oriental look. Bamboo also makes an effective hedge or barrier plant and can be frequently pruned to size and shape. A further advantage is that it can be grown in partial shade.

Banana shrub 含笑

Michela figo

Michela is closely related to the magnolias. *Michela figo* is a medium to large shrub grown for its cream-coloured flowers which have a fragrance reminiscent of bananas. The flowers appear in early summer but the shrub is also attractive for its dense foliage of dark green leaves. Small specimens may be cultivated in pots. Propagate by air layering.

Bauhinia (Hong Kong orchid tree) 洋紫荊

The **Hong Kong orchid tree** (洋紫荊, *Bauhinia blakeana*) is a beautiful medium-sized tree found everywhere in Hong Kong, cultivated in parks and roadsides, as well as growing wild in the hills. The tree was first discovered in 1908 growing by the seashore in Pokfulam by French missionary fathers near their mission house, "Bethany", which still stands today. By all accounts, these priests were talented botanists.

The tree is named after Sir Henry Blake, Governor of Hong Kong from 1898 to 1903. The large, purple, orchid-like flowers are best between October and April, but some flowers appear throughout the year.

B. blakeana has been the official floral emblem of Hong Kong since 1965. It is associated with all things to do with Hong Kong, and has assumed even greater eminence since the handover in 1997. A stylised bauhinia emblazoned on a red background is now the flag of the Special Administrative Region of Hong Kong.

This tree requires a lot of space and is not really suitable for a small garden. However, I have seen some decent-sized trees growing in large containers. *B. blakeana* very rarely produces any pods, and when it does, the seeds do not mature. If you see a bauhinia with lots of seed pods, it is not a *B. blakeana*. It is possible that this species is a sterile hybrid and can only be propagated by air layering.

The **camel's foot tree** (宮粉羊蹄, *B. variegata*) is so named because its leaves (in common with other bauhinias) are bi-lobed and resemble a hoof. It has light pink flowers and smaller leaves than *B. blakeana*. It also flowers at a different time, in spring and early summer. When in bloom it is easily recognisable because it is almost devoid of leaves, making a wonderful show. A white variety, *B. variegata* (var. Candida), retains its leaves even when flowering. Propagate by cuttings taken in spring.

The **purple camel's foot tree** (紅花羊蹄, *B. purpurea*) can be recognised for its flowering at an entirely different season from the others, namely in autumn. In spring it is laden with seed pods while the other species are in flower.

B. glauca (羊蹄甲籐) is a vigorous woody climber, white-flowered, quite common on our hillsides though not practical for home gardens.

Beans 豆類

A large variety of beans may be grown, mostly as summer crops. Sowing should begin in March through May. Cultivation is generally very similar for most types. Climbing beans will need support—a trellis, wigwam-type arrangement, open wire fence and so forth. Bush types and dwarf varieties can do without support.

Broad bean (蠶豆, *Vicia fabia*) is believed to be one of the earliest domesticated crop plants. It grows on an erect bush 30–60 cm high. The large pods contain four or five large flattened beans about 2.5 cm long. This is a cool-season crop.

French beans (扁豆, *Phaseolus vulgaris*) succeed well in local conditions and should be started in spring. There are climbing varieties and bush or dwarf varieties. I find the latter much more convenient to grow since no support or even staking is required. Most plants crop quite heavily and can even be pot-grown.

Garden peas (青豆, *Pisum sativum*) can be grown in summer but does better in cool weather. Seeds should be sown at the base of a support in October through December.

Lima beans

String beans

Lima beans (萊豆, *Phaseolus lunatis*) can be grown with equal success both in summer or winter. Again I prefer the bush varieties which may require some light staking. The beans resemble small broad beans and have a wonderful flavour.

Soy beans (黃豆, *Glycine max*) have been an important crop in China for five thousand years. Grow as a summer crop. It is an erect annual shrub about 50 cm high, producing hairy pods 4–8 cm long, each containing two to five rounded seeds. Its uses are legion and hardly need to be enumerated here.

String beans also known as yard-long or asparagus bean (豆角, *Vigna sesquipedalis*) is my favourite summer bean. It comes in two forms, the green and the white. The green variety is shorter, more slender, and generally superior in flavour and texture. The earlier green variety can be sown from March to May. If the spring is dull and damp, delay sowing until the weather brightens, or else growth will be slow. The white variety (actually a light green colour) should be sown later, from May to August. In fact, local farmers sometimes refer to this as "August beans" (八月豆). August, in this case, refers to the eighth month of the lunar year. A good idea is to grow them to follow the green variety, thus keeping up a continuous summer supply.

After preparing the ground, build a suitable trellis of bamboo for the vines to climb. Sow six seeds 2 cm deep at the base of each support. Later retain three healthy plants and thin out the rest. Keep the plants well watered in the summer heat, and feed once a week with dilute liquid fertiliser. As the mauve-coloured flowers appear, start thinning out the older leaves to prevent crowding and to give the flowers light and space. This thinning is very important and should be carried out every few days as long as beans are produced. The thinned-out leaves, by the way, can be eaten as greens. Though somewhat coarse in texture, they are quite palatable if thoroughly cooked. The flowers and young beans are very attractive to ants and this can cause poor cropping. Inspect regularly, washing off the ants or spraying with an organic pesticide if necessary. Harvest the green beans when they are about 35 cm long or when the beans within the pods just begin to swell. The white variety grows to about 45 cm.

Beetroot 紅菜頭

Beta vulgaris

Sow beetroot in the ground in October or November in drills 2 cm deep and 10 cm apart each way. Place three or four seeds in each drill and thin out later to retain the strongest seedling. Beets grow well locally but must have good drainage, a light soil, and regular feeding. Keep the soil loose around the plants and heap up sod over the enlarging globes as they grow.

Be careful though, not to injure the root while doing this, as it "bleeds" easily. Similar care should be exercised when harvesting. The vegetable is at its best when it reaches the size of a small orange.

Begonia 秋海棠科
Begonia sp.

This is a huge genus of about 9000 species of plants grown for their flowers or foliage. The first species was discovered in Brazil in 1690 by Charles Pluminer who named it after his patron, Michel Begon. As a group they are easily grown, shade-loving plants bearing male and female flowers on the same plant. The male flowers are generally the more showy, while the female flowers are readily distinguished by the prominent winged ovaries, which later develop into winged triangular seed capsules. The most suitable varieties for Hong Kong are of the **fibrous-rooted** group. The other two groups are the **rhizomatous-** and the **tuberous-rooted** begonias.

The fibrous-rooted ***Begonia semperflorens*** (蜆肉秋海棠 / 四季海棠) is the most popular and probably the easiest to grow. It is a much-branched dwarf species growing from 15–40 cm high, with succulent stems and thick, reddish green leaves. It grows best in partial shade, but unlike other begonias it is also tolerant of sun and so is a most versatile plant. Good drainage is essential and it should be watered only when the soil dries out. It is equally useful for garden beds and for verandah flower pots. Properly tended, this begonia will flower for most of the year. Start *B. semperflorens* from seed sown in October. Flowers begin appearing in March and continue until late May when most of the other autumn-grown flowering annuals have died away. Propagation by cuttings is equally effective. Take 7-cm cuttings of the growing shoots in October or March. Root in a mixture of peat moss and sand. Water thoroughly once, and do not water again until rooted. Grow on the rooted cuttings in a light soil with excellent drainage. After flowering, the plants should be discarded and replaced.

B. coccinea (茨姑秋海棠) is another member of the fibrous-rooted group. This shade-loving shrub grows to about 1 m in height. It is as attractive for its foliage as for its flowers. The large leaves are elongated, heart-shaped with a toothed margin. The upper surface is green, often spotted with white, and the under surface is a dark red. In the summer, large clusters of flowers in a rich shade of pink hang down gracefully. The female flowers are particularly notable for their winged ovaries. It is propagated with ease from either stem or leaf cuttings.

Originating in Mexico, ***B. rex*** (斑葉秋海棠) is a rhizomatous-rooted begonia grown mainly for its pretty variegated foliage. Pink flowers are also produced on mature plants.

Another group of begonias is the **tuberous-rooted begonias** (球根秋海棠) consisting almost entirely of hybrids. The leaves may die down in winter, re-emerging glossy-green in the spring. The flowers are large, showy, with many colours. Most have double flowers.

Bignonia (purple bignonia, trumpet flower) 比格諾籐
Bignonia magnifica

This vigorous, woody, climbing shrub from Brazil should be grown against a trellis or allowed to climb a fence with its strong, woody tendrils. In October or November, a profuse display of purple trumpet-shaped flowers with five spreading petals will appear. The flowers are clustered in bunches of 10 to 15. The display is impressive, especially in a large specimen, but lasts only two or three weeks. Occasionally a second, less profuse flowering will occur a few months later. It is best propagated by cuttings taken in spring or summer. It needs a moderate pruning in January.

Boston ivy (Virginia creeper) 爬牆虎
Parthenocissus himalayana

This very attractive deciduous climber from North America has become naturalised in Hong Kong where it is seen everywhere, climbing up walls and as ground cover. Its genus name is from the Greek *parthenos*, or "virgin", and *kissos*, meaning "creeper". It climbs by means of tiny adhesive discs that cling tenaciously to any available surface. The leaves vary in shape from cordate to trifoliate with transitional forms in between. It needs no care at all apart from trimming the edges to control its growth. During summer, the glossy-green leaves form a luxuriant, dense covering. In autumn, brilliant red, yellow, and brown hues appear before the leaves fall off for the winter. It is probably the best wall covering of all, especially for extensive areas. However, it may also climb up the rough bark of trees and eventually stifle them. Minute green-yellow flowers are borne in branched cymes 7–10 cm across. Dark blue berry-like fruits are borne in loose clusters. Propagation is easy with cuttings. Like *Hedera*, cuttings from young runner growth will produce a climbing habit, whereas cuttings from the mature sections will result in a less rampant, somewhat bushier growth.

Bougainvillea 葉子花、棘杜鵑、毛寶巾

Bougainvillea glabra—magenta

Bougainvilleas are natives of Brazil, and are vigorous climbers with a flamboyant show. They are probably the most popular of flowering climbers in Hong Kong, and deservedly so. Bougainvilleas are essentially scrambling shrubs, producing long canes with strong woody thorns that act as an aid to climbing. Properly pruned, they make excellent shrubs as well. The true flowers are small and inconspicuous but are surrounded by three colourful bracts, all appearing in large clusters to provide a glorious appearance. They need lots of sun and regular feeding. Purple, red, white, blue, orange and cream flowers, sometimes double, are all available. All bougainvilleas can be easily raised from cuttings any time of the year.

Bougainvillea glabra is probably the most familiar of the bougainvilleas. Typically the flowers are magenta, less commonly white. This variety grows vigorously, putting out long canes with curved thorns which make an excellent barrier to unwelcome visitors. *B. glabra* is always in good leaf, unlike some other varieties that lose their leaves periodically. It has two main flowering periods, in March / April and November / December, but flowers in smaller numbers appear almost throughout the year. After flowering the plants should be pruned to shape up for the next growing period. Do not hesitate to prune severely if necessary. Pruning a large specimen can be a tough job and its thorns need to be treated with respect. Nasty injuries can result otherwise, as the thorns are quite capable of penetrating the soles of rubber shoes. The thorns of dried, dead branches are even more lethal. Leather gloves are a sensible precaution.

B. spectabilis is also a vigorous climber, with red blossoms. *Bougainvillea* "San Diego Red" is a particularly showy hybrid with masses of red blossoms, often to the almost total exclusion of leaves. After the flowering period, these varieties benefit from a period of stress by dehydration. Allow new growth to be made after an initial pruning. When sufficient growth has occurred, withhold water up to a point when the leaves wither and begin to fall. This will take four or five days. Then water and feed heavily and wait for the next spectacular flowering show.

Bougainvillea glabra—white

Bougainvillea spectabilis

Broccoli 西蘭花

Brassica oleracea var. Italica

Broccoli is simply another variety of cauliflower though with much smaller heads. In taste though, it is much more similar to Chinese flowering kale or kai-lan (芥蘭). A second variety, **sprouting broccoli**, produces a large number of smaller, less dense curds. However, I have not seen it in Hong Kong, probably because it requires much cooler weather for satisfactory growth. The growing period of broccoli is quite long, about 90 days. Cultivation is similar to cauliflower.

Brunfelsia (Brazil lady-of-the-night, yesterday today and tomorrow) 鴛鴦茉莉

Brunfelsia calycina

This is a most attractive, slow-growing, medium-sized shrub, flowering freely from spring through summer. The flowers are rather simple, with a narrow tube flaring into five flat petals. They are a rich blue when they first appear, fading to a pale lavender, and then to white before they finally fall. The effect is a startling display of a bush with flowers of these different colours, all at the same time. The flowers produce a delightful fragrance at night. The shrub loses its leaves briefly in the winter at which time a light pruning to shape will be beneficial. It is easily propagated by cuttings taken in summer. Performs best in filtered sun and deserves to be more widely planted in Hong Kong. The plant contains poisonous alkaloids, and its berry-like fruits are known to have poisoned dogs.

Brussels sprouts 抱子甘藍株

Brassica oleracea var. Gemmifera

This delicious cool-season vegetable is seldom grown locally and the seeds are not always available. However, it does grow reasonably well in Hong Kong provided the winter is not too warm. The plants are large and have a long growing period, so keep just two or three in some part of the garden where they will not obstruct. If you do not have a garden, take heart, for they grow quite well in large containers, say 25-cm pots, one to a pot.

Sow the seeds from October to December and move the young seedlings to their final positions when 7 cm tall. Avoid over-watering. The growing plants are quite decorative when grown in pots. The sprouts appear on the main stem one to each leaf axil. The leaves should be removed from below as they begin to turn yellow. Harvest the sprouts when they are about the size of a large chestnut and when they are still tender. When the plants have reached the end of their growth the new leaves become bunched together like a small cabbage. This, together with the top 25 cm of the plant, can be cut off and eaten as greens.

Buddhist pine 羅漢松

Podocarpus macrophyllus

This is a particularly handsome evergreen shrub or tree which may reach a height of about 5 m. Its dense foliage is attractive all year round, each leaf resembling a flat needle about 5 cm long. The plant tolerates pruning well and can be manipulated to produce interesting shapes and forms. It is suitable also for screens and topiaries. An excellent pot plant, it prefers large containers. Grow in part shade, away from strong wind.

Bulbs 球莖

Broadly speaking, there are two groups of bulbs—those used for one season and then discarded, and those that can be retained to flower again and again. In the first group are narcissus, tulip, hyacinth, iris, crocus and daffodil. Gladiolus, for the purpose of the amateur gardener, is also best placed in this group.

The **narcissus** or **Chinese sacred lily** (水仙, *Narcissus tazetta*) is probably the best loved of all bulbs in Hong Kong and has special significance in the Chinese New Year. Production of narcissus bulbs is a highly specialised and lucrative industry. The bulbs appear on the market around December, and selecting a good bulb is no easy task. The wide range in prices may be a guide to the quality of the bulbs, but this is obviously not foolproof. It takes an experienced eye to determine the likely number of flowering shoots that a bulb will produce. The aim of cultivating narcissus is to have the plant in full flower on Chinese New Year Day. First, remove any attached bulblets that are deemed unlikely to produce flowering spikes. Then remove those that are in inconvenient positions such as to make proper placement of the bulb difficult. The next step is to carefully incise the bulb at strategic places so as to facilitate the emergence of the shoots. Generally, these incisions are placed after careful palpation to determine as far as possible where the hidden flowering shoots might be. The beginner will do well to consult a more experienced friend before taking this step.

The bulbs are placed in water, usually in a shallow decorative bowl specially designed for narcissus. Small pebbles help to keep the bulb in position. The bowl is placed in bright shade or part sun. As the spikes appear, it soon becomes evident whether or not they carry flowering heads. The amount of light or sun to which they are exposed more or less determines the rate of growth and it is interesting to observe if one's timing is correct. A good display on Chinese New Year's Day ensures good fortune for the coming year! It takes about 25 days from soaking to flowering. In an average season you will not be far wrong if you start soaking the bulbs on the fourth day of the twelfth moon in the Chinese lunar calendar.

Bulbs of **tulip**, **hyacinth**, **gladiolus** and **iris** are generally found in the shops in late autumn. They are useful only for one season and are then discarded. However, they provide a simple and quick method for colourful results. **Crocus** and **daffodil**, of such rugged habit in temperate climates, are not so easily available here, and again are used for a once-only show. The spent bulbs do not usually survive the hot Hong Kong summers.

The bulbs below form the second group, and do not need to be lifted as they survive into the next season.

The **blood lily** (網球花, *Scadoxus multiflorus*) is striking in appearance. The bulbs produce long ovate leaves and, in summer, a single stem topped by a dense umbel of numerous star-shaped flowers with long stamens. The flower head is enclosed in coloured bracts and the whole appearance resembles a powder puff or shaving brush. Blood lily is very suitable for pot culture.

Chinese amaryllis

I can also recommend **Chinese amaryllis**, also known as spider lily (忽地笑, *Lycoris aurea*), as a low-maintenance bulb that can be left in the ground throughout the year. The bright orange lilies are borne on tall solid stems which spring up in October before the appearance of leaves. They are great as cut flowers. Remove the stems as the flowers die. Sword-like leaves then develop to feed the bulbs throughout the winter after which they die down. During this growth period they should be kept well watered and regularly fed.

The **Easter lily** (麝香百合, *Lilium longiflorum*) is popular in pots and as cut flowers. Place four bulbs in a 25-cm pot in September and keep in shade until they begin to grow, then gradually accustom to the sun. It flowers in April. The bulbs can be left in the soil for the next season, although not all may survive. A wild form, ***L. brownii*** (淡紫百合) is quite commonly found on exposed hillsides, usually flowering somewhat later, in June. Large numbers can be found on Ma On Shan at this time.

Freesias (小蒼蘭, *Freesia* x *hybrida*) grow from corms, which are similar to bulbs. The many beautiful hybrids are easy to grow and their scented flowers are much appreciated. Useful as cut flowers, they also make attractive pot plants. In September / October, place four corms in a 21-cm pot so that the tips are just below the surface of the soil; then cover them with a 3-cm layer of peat. Flowers appear in spring. The corms multiply quite rapidly and the new corms are used for propagation. The spent corms may survive *in situ* until the next season, but a safer strategy is to lift them and store in dry sand until they are needed again. Freesias can also be successfully grown from seed, although taking five to six months to flower.

Hippeastrum

Perhaps my own favourite bulb is the ***Hippeastrum*** (花朱頂蘭), a genus of tropical and subtropical lilies, indigenous to South America. They are related to and often described as *Amaryllis* which is the old genus name. The bulbs are large with stout, strap-shaped leaves. Two to four flowers are carried on a robust hollow stem. The flowers are trumpet shaped, large (about 15 cm across) and very attractive. *Hippeastrum* has been intensely bred by the Dutch, and it is these developed hybrids that are most often grown. Colours vary, but the most common are white with radiating red stripes ("Candy cane") or red ("Kalahari").

Flowers appear in March or April after which water should be gradually withheld. The bulbs can be left *in situ* and will flower again the next year. Propagation is by offset bulbs which develop freely. Unlike many other bulbs, these should be planted close to the surface, with one third of the bulb exposed. It can also be raised from seed. However, with this method, it will not flower for the first three years. *Hippeastrum* has my strongest recommendation as it is ideal for Hong Kong and will thrive with very little care. Flowers from older bulbs tend to lose their colour progressively and should be replaced as necessary. *Hippeastrum* is very suitable for pot culture but re-potting will be needed every few years as the new bulbs crowd the pot. A sunny position is essential for the flowers to achieve good colour.

Zephyranthes candida

Zephyranthes grandiflora

Zephyranthes pulchella

Kaffir lily (君子蘭, *Clivia miniata*) belongs to the same *Amaryllidaceae* family as *Hippeastrum* and *Lycoris aurea*. It is particularly suited to pot culture. Its leaves are dark green, strap-shaped, 30–40 cm long. In spring, the stout flower stems bear 10–20 flowers in terminal umbels. Each flower is trumpet-shaped, orange-red with a yellow throat. The plant needs copious water and warmth in the flowering period but hot, direct sunlight should be avoided. Leave the bulbs in the pot at the end of the growth period and re-pot only when root-bound. Propagation is by careful division or from seed.

Zephyr flower (風雨花, *Zephyranthes*) also known as windflower or rain lily, is another care-free bulb. There are three species of this charming flower that are suitable for Hong Kong. Plant them in clumps, in rock gardens or odd corners. There is the pure-white *Z. candida*, the bright-yellow *Z. pulchella*, and the rich-pink *Z. grandiflora*. All are very similar, resembling the crocus, yet each has its separate characteristics. Zephyr flower grows from small bulbs, producing long slender leaves resembling chives. Flowers are carried singly on hollow stems and appear throughout the summer. The flowers close up in the evening.

All three species enjoy wet conditions, but *Z. grandiflora* in particular, tends to appear in profusion after heavy rains. It is the shortest of the three, at about 15 cm in height. *Z. pulchella*, the tallest of the three at about 20 cm, sets flat, black seeds routinely in large numbers. These can be collected for easy and reliable propagation. On the other hand, I have not observed *Z. candida* to set seed, and *Z. grandiflora* but rarely. However, they are readily propagated through offset bulbs which are produced in abundance. A reasonable amount of sunshine is required—about three or four hours a day.

Bush clockvine 硬枝老鴨嘴

Thunbergia erecta

This semi-deciduous, much-branched small shrub is named after the eighteenth century Swedish botanist, Carl Peter Thunberg, who collected this species from Africa. It has settled comfortably in Hong Kong and deserves to be more widely grown. Throughout the summer it produces a profusion of trumpet-shaped flowers of deep purple contrasting with a bright yellow throat. It has a rugged habit, and much growth is made in a year. It grows best in partial sun but will also grow happily in open shade. Left unattended, it will tend to climb if there is nearby support, even though it has none of its own climbing accessories such as tendrils or thorns. If grown as a shrub it benefits from a hard annual pruning in February. If grown as a hedge, then simply prune as required for shape and size control anytime in spring or summer. This plant does well in ordinary soil and overfeeding will result in a profusion of foliage and fewer flowers. Cuttings succeed routinely in spring and summer.

Cabbage 椰菜
Brassica oleracea var. Capitata

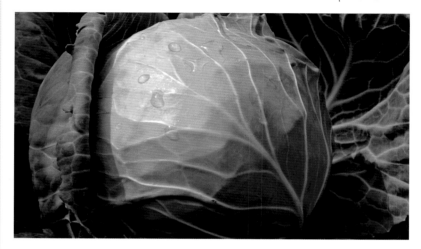

Brassica is a remarkable genus that produces a greater range of important vegetables than any other. This favourite vegetable takes three to four months to mature, though some early varieties can be ready in two or three months. As it takes up quite a lot of room for such a long growing period it is not very popular in small gardens. However, I think it is well worth growing as the end product is so satisfying. Besides, cabbages can grow successfully in 21-cm pots, producing solid, mouth-watering heads of 1 kg or more. Pot-grown plants are also very decorative.

Seeds can be sown September to November, four seeds to a 7-cm plastic pot. Germination takes place in about four days. When the second leaves appear, the seedlings should be thinned to retain the strongest plant. Add soil as necessary to cover the spindly stalks which might otherwise keel over. Plant out in their final positions when about 10 cm tall, in soil that has been heavily fertilised. Cabbage grows best in a lime-rich, moist, well-drained soil. Ideally they should be 60 cm apart, but if space is limited they can do quite well a mere 30 cm apart. Otherwise, plant one to a 21-cm pot. Feed every two weeks with a suitable fertiliser—peanut cake is particularly effective. Cabbage, like all *Brassicas*, is more prone to pests and diseases than most vegetables, and insecticides are difficult to avoid if perfect, undamaged vegetables are required. However, in a small garden it should be possible to inspect the plants regularly to detect cabbage worms which should be picked out by hand and destroyed. Remove the outer leaves as they turn yellow. Harvest when the heads feel solid or when the new outer leaves begin to split. The outer coarse green leaves need not be discarded as they can be removed from time to time and used to prepare an excellent vegetable soup.

Cabbage, Chinese 黃芽白
Brassica pekinensis

Grow this in the same way as cabbage. It grows more quickly, but each plant occupies a little more space. As the cabbage grows, its leaves tend to splay out to present themselves to the available sunlight. At this point, it is necessary to tie up the plant to encourage inward growth of the leaves as well as to blanch them. Undo the ties from time to time in order to inspect for worms. These should be picked out by hand and destroyed. Snails can also be an annoying problem. Avoid over-watering which can cause rotting of the heads. Harvest when the heart is tight and well formed.

Caladium (elephant's ears) 彩葉芋

Caladium bicolor

This genus of tuberous-rooted perennials is much prized for their colourful foliage. The leaves are shaped like arrowheads and come in various mixes of green, white and red. Some are prominently etched with a striking pattern of veins. They form an interesting display if different coloured species are planted in a mixture.

In spring, caladium can be planted in the ground or in pots. It prefers partial shade. Excessive shade produces long stems with poorly coloured leaves. The colourful display lasts throughout the summer. Water frequently and feed every two weeks with a liquid fertiliser. After the leaves die down in autumn, put the pots away and keep them dry in the winter. Ground-grown tubers may be left in but must be kept dry. In spring, moisten the soil and keep it damp until the first shoots emerge. Thereafter water generously. Propagation is by division of the tubers or by detachment of the offsets as they appear in spring.

Calendula (pot marigold) 金鐘

Calendula officinalis

A garden favourite, best grown as an autumn-sown annual from September onwards. If planted in spring, it flowers in early summer and so is a valuable stopgap between winter and summer annuals.

Camellia 茶花

Camellia japonica

The common camellia is an evergreen shrub with stiff dark green leaves and showy blooms appearing in winter and early spring. Originating in Japan and China, endless varieties have been produced under cultivation. The flowers are most commonly pink, sometimes red or white and sometimes variegated. Camellias require rich, well-drained soil with a high organic content. The plant is an acid lover and does best with liberal applications of peat moss or a commercial acid feed. However, do not overfeed as this will cause leaf drop or spotting. Keep the soil moist but never soggy. Camellias do well in the sun or partial shade but should be sheltered from the hot summer afternoon sun. Keep out of strong winds. Dead-head after flowering. No regular pruning is required as the bush is of a slow growing habit. A lean plant may, however, need pruning for shaping or to revitalise it. The pruning cuts should be made just above the scar marking where the previous year's growth has stopped and the new growth begins.

Camellia sinensis is the plant from which comes all the world's tea. It is now grown in the highlands of tropical Asia, southern China, Japan and other parts of the world where the climate is sufficiently warm and humid. Its tender new shoots can be hand-picked, fermented and dried to produce black or green tea.

Canna (Indian shot) 美人蕉

This is a truly tropical-looking, robust, rhizomatous perennial, native to South America. It belongs to the same broad grouping as the gingers and bananas, and resembles these in that the apparent above-ground stems are tightly furled leaf bases growing from a rhizomatous rootstock. Flowering stalks, 1 m high, grow up through the centre of these apparent stems to bear large rather floppy-looking flowers, which may be red, orange, pink or yellow in colour. Flowers appear in succession in summer. Many garden cannas are *Canna* x *generalis* hybrids with a wide range of colours. Usually propagated by division of the rootstock where shoots appear, though *C. indica* can also be raised from seed.

Cantaloupe (musk melon) 蜜瓜

Cucumis melo

This can be grown successfully in summer. The vines are not very large and can be grown in 30-cm pots. In fact, it is a good idea to use containers so that they can be taken to shelter when the inevitable typhoons strike.

In April, place a stout 1 m long bamboo support in the middle of a 30-cm pot and plant four seeds around its base. Thin out to retain the strongest seedling. Feed with a liquid fertiliser every four weeks. Keep well watered without wetting the foliage. Pay particular attention to the mulching of pot-grown plants to prevent drying out. These plants thrive in the heat and humidity of our summer. They will not do well in shade and require full sun. When the main stem reaches the top of the support, stop the growth. Secondary laterals bear the male and female flowers. The latter are easily recognisable by the swelling beneath the blossom. Although not absolutely necessary, hand pollination is recommended. Pick a male flower, remove its petals and smear the pollen into the centre of the female flower. Not more than two fruits should be allowed to mature on any one plant. Keep the fruits from touching the soil, and as they increase in weight, a light net support should be rigged up. The ripening fruits are popular with sucking insects and birds, so some protection against them must be mounted. A melon is ready for picking when it begins to turn yellow and when the stem begins to crack away from the fruits. At this time it also gives off a delicious fruity aroma best detected by sniffing the blossom end.

Capsicum 辣椒 / 燈籠椒 / 牛角椒

A genus of many species of small shrubs—annuals, or treated as such. *Capsicum annum* provides all the variations in size and shape of the genus as a whole, from the bell peppers for salads to the smallest and hottest of chillies. The cultivars form three broad groups. The **Grossum** group includes the main salad peppers, pimento and sweet peppers. The **Longum** group includes the banana peppers, elongated and often curved, mildly hot. The **Conoides** group has conical fruit, usually small

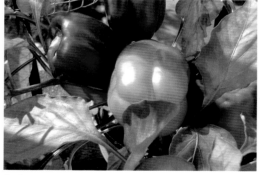

Bell peppers

and very hot. Many in this group are beautifully coloured and used as ornamental pot plants. Some of the capsicums grown locally are *C. frutescens*. These can be distinguished from *C. annum* by having two or more flowers in each leaf axil. The fruits are usually small and very hot. The famous Tabasco sauce is made from a strain named after a town of this name in southern Mexico. However, the hottest chilli on earth is said to be the habanero, a squat, small, innocuous-looking orange-coloured fruit that is about fifty times hotter than its nearest rival. Try this deadly capsicum only if you have resuscitation equipment handy!

Sow seeds from September through October. Prick out the seedlings into transplanting boxes, pans or into small individual plastic pots. Move into 21-cm pots when 10 cm high, one to a pot. Alternatively, sow seeds directly in the 21-cm pot and thin to retain the strongest seedling. A sunny position is best. Feed with a liquid fertiliser or peanut cake once a fortnight. Chillies may also be sown in spring and throughout the summer, but bell peppers do better in cooler weather. Capsicum leaves may also be eaten. They are best used for a light soup in much the same way as one would use matrimony vine (see that section). In fact, the taste is almost identical.

Capsicum is the source of capsaicin, a molecule found in the white "rib" of hot chillies. This molecule has been shown to have pain-killing properties and is now available in many topical lotions and creams for pain relief in arthritis, inflammation, insect bites and so on. Capsaicin is believed to be part of the plant's defence mechanism. However, it is certainly no defence against certain birds, especially crested mynahs, who have a special liking for the hottest, ripest chillies. They can wipe your crop out in a few minutes. If mynahs are active in your area, consider some form of protection such as netting.

If you have a surplus of hot chillies, try preserving some in vinegar, or else soak some in soy sauce for future use. Or why not make some home-made chilli sauce? My office cleaning lady keeps me in constant supply with her own special chilli sauce, the recipe of which she has kindly agreed to share with us.

Chilli sauce 辣椒油

<u>Ingredients</u>

- 250 g hot chillies, finely chopped
- 3 cloves garlic, finely chopped
- 50 g dried shrimps, soaked in water for 10 mins., then finely chopped
- 1 tsp. five-spice powder
- 250 mL peanut oil
- 50 mL sesame oil
- 30 mL light soy sauce
- Salt and pepper

<u>Method</u>

- Stir-fry separately, in a little hot oil, the garlic, shrimps and chillies. Do not allow the garlic to brown.
- Mix the three ingredients, and continue to stir-fry on low heat, while adding the peanut oil a little at a time. The five-spice powder is also added a little at a time, then the salt and pepper and the soy sauce. After about 15 mins., all the oil should have been added. Now stir in the sesame oil and the job is done.
- Store in little bottles and distribute to all your friends.

Carrot 甘筍
Daucus carota

A great garden favourite, long on flavour and packed with vitamins. The carrot is believed to have originated in Afghanistan and introduced into Europe about six hundred years ago. Carrots may be short, medium or long rooted. I find a medium-length variety such as "Nantes" works best locally, though the growing period is long, about a hundred days. A single sowing allows a supply of six to eight weeks if the roots are carefully pulled. Carrots should be grown in light, well-cultivated soil, free of stones. Prepare the soil by digging down to at least 30 cm, breaking up clods and mixing in a generous amount of peat moss and well-matured compost. If necessary, further lighten the soil with coarse sand or perlite. Do not use rough, fresh compost as this will cause forking of the roots. Carrots do best in a sunny site but will also succeed in part shade.

Carrot seeds should always be sown where they are to grow. The first sowing can be made in early September. However, carrot seeds are small and the germinating seedlings very delicate. After having my early-sown carrots wiped out repeatedly by September rains, I now delay planting until October. Sow the seeds 1 cm deep and 1 cm apart, in rows which should be about 12 cm apart. Fresh seeds germinate in about a week, but do not be impatient as it sometimes takes about twice this time. Keep thinning out the seedlings as they begin to crowd, eventually ending with roots about 5 cm apart. The later thinnings will in fact be miniature carrots which can be eaten raw or used in salads. Water regularly and do not allow drying out. Irregular watering causes roots to split as the dehydrated roots literally burst open when water eventually becomes available. Carrots can be pulled when the top end of the root is about 3 cm across. Thereafter pull them as required for the next few weeks.

Cassia

Winged cassia

This genus comprises about a hundred shrubs and trees from tropical and subtropical regions throughout the world. The **sunshine tree** (黃槐, *Cassia surrattensis*) is perhaps the commonest in Hong Kong. Quick-growing and vigorous, it produces racemes of 15–20 flowers throughout the summer, and sporadically at other times. A very common tree in parks and roadsides, perhaps also suitable for a small garden.

I can highly recommend the **winged cassia** (有翅決明, *C. alata*). It will grow to a fair size in a planter or even a medium-sized container. Erect spikes of bright yellow flowers appear throughout the summer. Like *C. surrattensis*, the leaves are characteristic: pinnate, alternate, with 10–20 pairs of leaflets. The fruit is a ridged pod containing a large number of seeds which may be used for propagation. Note, however, that the woody branches of all cassias are very brittle and often suffer damage from strong winds unless properly supported and tethered. The plant is the source of chrysophanic acid, which is used to treat some skin diseases.

Cat's claw climber 貓爪藤
Doxantha unguis-cati

This very attractive climber is occasionally seen in Hong Kong gardens and deserves more attention. It is best displayed when allowed to ramble extensively on a fence which it will drape with yellow flowers every July. The flowers do not last long though, perhaps four weeks. The flowers are single or in small clusters, bright yellow, trumpet-shaped with five petals. It closely resembles the purple bignonia, as they belong, after all, to the same family. It is a vigorous climber, gaining purchase on any support by tenacious tendrils at the ends of the leaves. The fruit is a long bean-like capsule up to 25 cm long, containing numerous seeds which scatter as the capsules burst. Propagation is by seed or cuttings.

Cauliflower 椰菜花
Brassica oleracea var. Botrytis

Though not popular in local gardens, it is not difficult to obtain specimens of respectable size. Generally they are treated in the same way as cabbage, to which same family they belong. Cauliflower occupies quite a lot of space, so it may be a good idea to grow them in large containers rather than to take up valuable ground space. Cultivate the soil regularly, filling up and firming the soil around each plant. Water freely and do not allow any setback in growth. Like cabbage, it is a heavy feeder. When the curds appear, allow them to grow to about 10 cm in diameter, and then tie up the outer leaves to blanch the curds. Loosen the ties from time to time to check on growth and pests. When the curds are round and full, harvest promptly.

Celery 西芹

Apium graveolens

This popular salad vegetable is grown for its tight cluster of crescent-sectioned stalks. It is a cool weather vegetable and seeds should be sown from October to November. The growing period is relatively long, taking about 120 or more days to maturity. In order that it does not occupy valuable ground space for this length of time, it is useful to know that celery may be conveniently grown in pots, one plant to a 21-cm pot. Remove any basal shoots that spring up from time to time. The traditional way to keep the stalks blanched is to earth up the plants. I find this a totally unnecessary and burdensome step, and prefer simply to grow the plants quickly, leaving the stalks to turn a light green colour. Some self-blanching varieties are available from specialist vendors. This vegetable is not difficult to grow although I have never been able to produce stalks as thick and crunchy as store-bought celery. Perhaps our weather is too warm.

Chinese celery

Another variety of celery, which I tend to grow more of these days, is **Chinese celery** (芹菜, *Apium graveolens L.* var. Dulce DC). It has thin, fibrous stalks, not suitable for eating raw. However, it has a much stronger taste than the salad variety, and is therefore better for flavouring stews and soups and for stir-fry. These plants are much more slender than salad celery and can be grown closely together in beds or eight plants to a 21-cm pot. Growing the plants in close proximity to each other results in tall, slender stalks and self-blanching from exclusion of strong light. A simple, reliable recipe for cream of celery soup follows.

Cream of Chinese celery soup 芹菜忌廉湯

Ingredients

- Bunch of Chinese celery (about 200 g)
- One large potato
- 500 mL chicken stock
- 1000 mL water
- 4 tbs. corn starch
- 200 mL evaporated milk
- 1/3 bar brown (slab) sugar
- Salt and pepper

Method

- Roughly chop the celery and cook in 700 mL water until soft. Retain the water.
- Remove the celery to a blender, add 300 mL cold water and blend thoroughly.
- Pass the blended celery into the retained water through a sieve to remove the fibre.
- Peel the potato, cook till soft, then blend in a little cold water. Add the blended potato into the soup.
- Mix the corn starch with cold water and stir into the soup.
- Add the stock, bring to a boil and simmer for 10 mins.
- Add the seasoning, brown sugar and the evaporated milk last of all.

C

Ceylon spinach 潺菜

Basella rubra L. var. Alba

Ceylon spinach is one of the rare successful leafy vegetables in summer. It is an annual or biennial climber but is usually harvested before it begins to climb. The leaves are characteristically fleshy with a slightly slimy sap which is reflected in its Chinese name which means "mucilaginous vegetable". Sow the seeds from April to September in the soil where they are to grow. They may be transplanted into rows but I usually skip this laborious step in favour of just thinning the plants as necessary. The leaves are very good for a simple, light summer soup. Bring some chicken stock to a boil, and then toss in a good handful of leaves. Bring back to the boil, add a beaten egg and, presto, the soup is done.

Champak (pak lan) 白蘭

Michelia alba

A tree growing to about 10 m or more in height. Young trees are popular as pot plants and a good specimen can be grown in a 30-cm pot. A dragon urn is even better. The trees can be kept small by regular pruning. Champak is grown for its fragrant white flowers which appear in spring and continue sporadically throughout the summer. The scent is arguably the sweetest and most pleasant of any plant in Hong Kong. The flowers appear singly, in the leaf axils. Each flower is about 3 cm long and is wrapped in a tough, brown bract which falls off before the flower opens. The flowers may be picked just as they begin to open when they are at their most fragrant. Flowers are used to perfume interiors or to wear in women's hair. Taxi drivers use them to freshen their cabs (also ginger lily). It sheds some, but seldom all of its leaves in winter. New leaves appearing in spring are popular with caterpillars which should be sought out and destroyed.

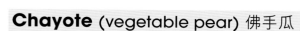
Chayote (vegetable pear) 佛手瓜

Sechium edule

This large, wide-spreading vine grows rapidly. It grows from thick, tuberous roots and has three- to five-lobed leaves with minute teeth. The fruit is light green, about the shape and size of a pear, and slightly bumpy. Very large numbers can be produced from a single vine provided it has the space to expand. The fruit contains a single seed and a mature fruit is planted whole to start the vine. It is best planted as a summer vegetable, around April. The difficulty is in finding a mature fruit, since any sprouting fruit would normally be thrown away. A diligent search in the wet markets will occasionally turn one up, and the vendor will be only too happy to flog it off to the "foolish" customer. It is said to be eaten raw in salads in Central America, but in Hong Kong, the fruit is usually eaten cooked when it has a resemblance to papaya. It may be stir-fried or used in soup with a meat or fish base.

Chenille plant (red-hot cat-tail) 狗尾紅

Acalypha hispida

A small shrub, thought to be from Malaysia, producing in summer tiny flowers in long, red, tassel-like spikes growing from the leaf axils. The leaves are broadly oval, 15 cm long, 8 cm wide, slightly hairy and unfortunately quite popular with mealy bugs and red spider mites. A very useful pot plant for the hot summer months, though not one of my favourites. Raise from tip cuttings in March. Grow in a sheltered site with partial sun. The plants branch and become bushy naturally and do not require pinching out of the growing tips. It is best to raise new plants each year, discarding the old growth.

There is some disagreement between the English and Chinese common names—the one invokes the tail of a cat while the other opts for the dog.

Chinese spinach 莧菜

Amaranthus tricolor

You will note that *Amaranthus tricolor* will appear lower down the list under "Joseph's coat". This delicious vegetable is simply one of the many strains of this plant and is grown for the table and not for ornament. It is especially important as it becomes available in the summer when other leafy greens are scarce.

Of rapid growth habit, it is ready for the table six to eight weeks from sowing. Sow the seeds in the ground from March to July. The seeds are very small and mixing with fine sand before sowing will help to achieve even distribution. Rake the soil lightly then press the earth down gently. There is no need to cover the seed with a layer of soil. A superstition exists about Chinese spinach that after sowing, one must not dust one's hands by clapping them together. So doing creates an ill wind that prevents germination. I don't believe this to be true, but I also find myself unable to tempt fate. Germination takes place in about three days in pleasing profusion, but the tiny seedlings are a favourite with birds which may wipe out the whole bed in a day. Being a summer crop, seedlings are also vulnerable to heavy rainstorms. Assuming the birds and the rain have been kept away, begin thinning when about 5 cm high. The mature plants are usually pulled out completely and are sold in the markets in this way, roots and all. However, the home gardener need not be so wasteful. The vegetable can be cut to leave a few axillary shoots to spring forth. At least three generations can be expected and the supply kept up for weeks. This is especially practical for the verandah gardener who grows in pots. Five pots can provide quite a few meals. However, if sowing is done in pots, remember not to sow too thickly.

A wild variety of Chinese spinach *A. viridis* (野莧 / 馬屎莧) is very widespread. Because it self-seeds prodigiously, it is usually regarded as a weed. Nevertheless, it is a very tasty vegetable in its own right, especially in the making of soup, partiturally with fish and tofu. It occasionally appears in small amounts in wet markets. I make it a point to leave some growing in my kitchen garden all the time.

Wild Chinese spinach

Choi sum (Chinese flowering cabbage) 菜心
Brassica parachinensis

By far and away the most popular local vegetable, abundant in the winter months. Sow the seeds thinly in pans or in the ground from September to December. When the plants are 10 cm high, transplant to rows, keeping a distance of 15 cm each way. Keep the base of the young plants well covered with soil. Feed weekly with a dilute liquid fertiliser and harvest just as the flowers begin to open. Watch out for aphids. Cut the plants cleanly with a sharp knife, leaving two or three side shoots to produce a second picking.

It is important to purchase the correct seed for the particular time of year. In September sowings, the early variety, maturing in 40 days, should be planted. When buying seed, ask for the "40-day choi sum". In October/November, as the temperature falls, sow the 50- or 60-day variety, and in December the 70- or 80-day variety. If in doubt, ask for advice from the vendor. One type, known as the "yellow-leaved choi sum" (黃葉菜心), can be sown up to May, being tolerant of hot and humid conditions. However, the quality of the winter vegetable is much higher.

Christmas cactus (crab cactus, claw cactus) 蟹爪蘭
Zygocactus truncatus

This makes a striking pot plant. Its densely branching stems are made of jointed flat segments 3–5 cm long with a prominent midrib. It blooms during the Christmas season, hence its name. The flowers are exotic-looking, in various shades of red. They are unusual for cactus flowers in that they are not symmetrical, much in the same way as a snapdragon or pea flower is not symmetrical. Each flower lasts a few days only, but as buds are generally very numerous, the flowering period covers many weeks.

A novel form of the plant involves grafting a Christmas cactus onto the top of an erect single-stemmed cactus such as *Hylocereus*. This converts an otherwise sprawling plant into a stately specimen with the drooping branches creating an attractive "weeping" look. Grow Christmas cactus in open shade, away from the direct rays of the sun. The winter flowering process is initiated by the onset of shortening days, hence do not keep the plant indoors where night lighting may create artificially long days. Water freely in the growing period and tail off after flowering. It is easily raised by cuttings anytime in spring or summer.

Chrysanthemum 菊花

Chrysanthemum molifolium

Chrysanthemum morifolium is the most familiar form of chrysanthemum, the so-called "florist's chrysanthemum". However, even this produces many variations in flower form and size, from full, bushy blooms, to single daisy-like forms, to tiny pompoms.

Chrysanthemums are not difficult to grow but are difficult to grow well. Take cuttings in January, selecting healthy stems from the base of a flowering shoot. Cuttings usually root easily. Pot the rooted cuttings in early spring and feed two or three times during the growing season. Strategic pinching out is the secret of success. Begin at potting time, removing the tip of the new plant. Select two to four of the lateral shoots for continued growth, staking the plants to keep them upright. Continue pinching off every new shoot after it reaches 10 cm in length. As the sprays of buds appear, remove all buds except for one or two in each cluster. This is known as disbudding. When buds form, feed every week until flowers appear.

Marguerites, or *C. frutescens*, are best started with tip cuttings in September. The cuttings do not take so easily as *C. morifolium*, but keep trying. Marguerites again illustrate how difficult it is to grow chrysanthemums well. The old traditional Hong Kong gardeners, experts in container gardening, will pinch out the growing tips, peg down several branches, and produce a neat, dome-shaped display in spring. I have not yet been able to achieve this.

Chrysanthemum vine (crown daisy) 茼蒿

Chrysanthemum coronarium

This cool season vegetable should be started in October through to December. The leaves are deeply lobed and have a slightly herbal, distinctive taste. The plants are picked whole, when still young—about 10 cm high. Best eaten stir-fried or as part of a hot-pot meal when it is simply blanched in boiling water or soup. If left to grow on, it will ramble widely, producing quite pretty simple chrysanthemum flowers.

Cleome (spider flower) 醉蝶花

Cleome spinosa

This attractive bushy annual grows to a height of 1–1.5 m with clusters of pink flowers which are produced continuously as the flowering stem lengthens. The pink flowers have four narrow petals and long spidery stamens. The leaves are palmate with five to seven leaflets. The whole plant sometimes gives off a slightly pungent though not unpleasant odour. In full sun the flowers appear paler, while in the early morning and twilight they seem to be a richer colour with sharper contrast between the dark and pale areas. This is a very useful plant for Hong Kong as it grows easily, producing flowers continuously for two or three months. Because it is quite tall, it can be grown as a background to smaller plants.

Sow the seeds from September to November, either where they are to grow or in pans to be transplanted later. Full sun is required, together with a rich soil with good drainage. The plants often self-seed and will appear again the following year if the ground is not disturbed too much.

Clerodendron 馬鞭草科

Clerodenron sp.

Clerodendron is a very large genus of over four hundred species from the warmer parts of the globe. Three of these species are commonly found in Hong Kong.

Bleeding hearts (龍吐珠, *C. thomsoniae*) is a climbing shrub but it is seldom seen in this form since it is mostly used as a pot plant. In early summer, clusters of deep red flowers emerge from white, bell-shaped calyces. The leaves are deep green and form a contrasting background to the blooms. Grown against a trellis, it climbs easily, and is a very pretty sight in full flower. However, it may be difficult to maintain from year to year. At the end of the flowering period it should be severely cut back. New plants may be raised from cuttings started in February.

The **pagoda flower** (頹桐, *C. kaempferi*) has erect woody stems growing singly to about 1 m high. The leaves are heart-shaped and large, about 15 cm across. The flowers are bright scarlet, arranged in a long panicle, tapering at the top and, therefore, resembling a pagoda. It is a good plant to know about because it thrives in deep shade. It is a common sight in public gardens, usually grown under the shade of trees. It flowers throughout the summer and should be cut down severely at the end of the flowering period. The one problem, though, is that it spreads relentlessly through underground horizontal roots and is thus liable to take over from other desirable plants nearby. Propagation by cuttings is very easy. I grow them in 25-cm pots which I sink in the ground, thereby controlling their invasive habit.

Pagoda flower

The **glorybower** (紅龍吐珠, *C. splendens*) is a handsome climber with a long-lasting display of red flowers beginning in early winter. Left on its own it can be quite rampant, and a lot of leaf growth is made in a season. For this reason, it needs a sheltered site and needs trimming from time to time. Cuttings take with difficulty, and it is better to start from new suckers produced at the base of the plant.

Clitoria (butterfly pea) 蝶豆

Clitoria ternate

This is a hairy vine that climbs by twining itself around any nearby support. It bears pretty blue flowers with a bright yellow throat. As to its form, well, the eighteenth century taxonomist who named this plant was obviously not bashful about intimate female anatomy. The fruit is a pod with a long pointed end, containing about eight to ten black seeds which are poisonous. The plant is easily raised from seed sown in spring. Self-seeding is usual, and sometimes it can assume pest proportions. I avoid this problem by keeping only one plant going, confined to a pot, at the base of a lamppost which it graces every year with its pinnate leaves and attractive flowers.

Cockscomb/Chinese woolflower

Celosia argentea

This native of tropical Asia is a mainstay of colour in the hot summers. The species is best known by two cultivars whose appearances are similar until the flowers develop. When that happens, it is difficult to believe they are the same species. *Celosia argentea cristata* (雞冠花) produces flowers that fit the descriptive name of cockscomb, resembling, as it does, an exuberant cock's comb. The flowers are fan-shaped, velvety, contorted and fluted, in yellow, red, orange or purple. *C. argentea plumosa* (鳳尾球) produces bushy plumes consisting of dense clusters of very small flowers, red, yellow or purple resembling a clump of wool—hence, woolflower.

The small shiny black seeds are sown in pans as soon as the weather warms up in March or April. The *plumosa* group should be sown a little later—in June or July. The seeds are sown on the surface and just covered with a layer of fine soil. Prick off the seedlings into boxes and grow on till they are 5 cm tall when they can be planted in beds or in pots. A 21-cm pot will take two *cristata* seedlings or one of the bushier *plumosa* varieties. Growth is generally trouble-free, and these plants will grow in part shade. A lot of seeds are produced at the end of the flowering period and these may be collected and stored for the following season.

Coleus 洋紫蘇

Coleus blumei

Although there are over a hundred species, only *Coleus blumei* is usually grown. This is one of the most colourful and reliable plants to grow in Hong Kong. Although a shrubby perennial, it is not worth growing beyond one season, and new plants should be raised each year from seeds or cuttings. Coleus is grown for its striking foliage which comes in many shades of red, green, yellow and maroon. Some are beautifully variegated. In late summer, spikes of small two-lipped blue and white flowers are produced. More usually, though, the flowers are pinched out before they develop in order to encourage a bushy plant. Though mostly seen as pot plants, coleus is effective in beds or when used for ground cover, especially if different coloured plants are grown in a mix.

Seeds may be sown in spring. Select a seed collection of mixed colours and await the delightful surprise of the many varieties that appear. Cuttings are even easier than seeds. Take 7-cm cuttings of the growing tips, removing all except the last two leaves, anytime in spring or summer. They never fail to root, even in ordinary garden soil, provided they are not allowed to dry out. When the plants have picked up growth, pinch out the growing points to encourage bushy growth. Coleus performs best in open shade or filtered sun and is an ideal pot plant for the verandah. Some varieties have a trailing habit and are useful for hanging pots or baskets. With sufficient light, it also succeeds indoors. It always fails in excessive shade. In its period of active growth, coleus demands heavy watering and wilts easily in the hot summer sun. As growth slows down in the autumn, over-winter a few plants to provide cuttings for the next season.

Copper leaf 紅桑
Acalypha wilkesiana

A common cultivated shrub from Fiji, much-branched and bushy, growing up to 1.5 m in height. Now hugely popular in parks and gardens. It is grown for its attractive copper-coloured leaves splotched with green, red and brown. The leaves are ovate with scalloped edges. It produces its best colours only in full sun. Tiny male flowers without petals are produced in drooping, narrow catkins. Note that copper leaf is closely related to the chenille plant *Acalypha hispida* (狗尾紅) which has similar, drooping catkins. Female flowers are borne on the same plant in erect spikes. Cut back yearly as required to control growth. Overgrown plants are best discarded and new plants raised from cuttings in spring. Recently a green and white cultivar ('Godseffiana') of this plant has become very popular and is now seen in many parts of Hong Kong.

Cornflower 矢車菊
Centaurea cyanus

This is one of the best known of wildflowers in Europe, belonging to the thistle group of composites, and commonly occurring as a weed among wheat crops. It is an erect, branched annual with weak stems, grey-green leaves and flowers that prove their relation with thistles. Cultivated varieties have been produced in pink, white or purple, but none as attractive as the original blue. Both tall and compact varieties are available. They are good flowers for cutting. Seeds can be saved for the following season. Grow cornflower as an autumn-sown annual, in October, directly into the growing site. Cultivation is usually trouble-free.

Cosmos (Mexican aster) 秋英 / 波斯菊
Cosmos bipinnatus

This native of Mexico is a bright, cheerful, daisy-like flower with brittle, weak stems, and finely cut, delicate foliage. It grows to 1 m and is easily damaged by high winds. Some staking is usually necessary. Flowers are white, rose, purple or pink. The less common *Cosmos sulphureus* has orange blossoms, sometimes double.

Cosmos does best when sown in October but spring planting in March/April will succeed in providing much needed colour in the garden for those hot, early summer months. Grow in a bright, sunny spot. Too-rich soil produces foliage at the expense of flowers. Keep the soil just damp and dead-head to prolong flowering. Cosmos is a good pot plant.

Crepe (or crape) **myrtle** 紫薇
Lagerstroemia indica

A deciduous woody shrub or small tree, widely grown in Hong Kong gardens and parks. The branches are long and slender with little branching. In summer, large conical clusters of flowers are produced at the end of the slightly drooping branches. The flowers are showy, crinkled and crepe-like in pink, mauve or white. It is a valuable source of summer colour in the garden and grows easily in any sunny site. Even in part shade it performs well. In February it must be pruned right down to the old wood. The prunings may be cut into 10-cm sections and rooted in ordinary garden soil. Few cuttings take with greater ease. In fact, I have sometimes used the long twiggy prunings as support for other plants, only to find a few weeks later that these supports have rooted. Cuttings cannot come any easier than that!

Croton 變葉木
Codiaeum variegatum

This one species alone has given rise to a large number of cultivars of ornamental shrubs grown for their colourful foliage. They can also be grown as small trees. There are wide variations in the forms and colours of the leaves, which range from ovate to lobed to linear,

and combinations of green, yellow, red, orange, pink and black. Some have fancy, wavy or twisted leaves. They are very popular as pot plants and grow best in filtered sun. Excessive shade results in less vivid colours. These plants generally thrive without much care. No pruning is required except to shape or to revitalise a rangy specimen. Growth slows down markedly in the winter when some leaf drop may occur. Grows easily from tip cuttings.

Cucumber 青瓜

Cucumis sativus

Sow cucumber seeds in March. Plant four seeds to a drill, 2 cm deep at the base of a trellis, fence or suitable support. Thin out the seedlings to leave the strongest plant. Cultivation is similar to hairy squash, and the reader is referred to that section.

Cuphea (false heather, Mexican heather, cigar flower) 萼距花屬

Cupheas are shrubby perennials of compact growth, with much-branched weak stems, and small, simple leaves. Flowers are very small and very numerous, appearing throughout the year.

False or **Mexican heather** (細葉萼距花, *Cuphea hyssopifolia*) closely resembles heather. When I told my one-time neighbour Jack that it was not really heather, he insisted it *was* heather, adding with a huff that, as a Scotsman, he should know! Its tiny flowers are short tubes with colourful purple petals giving a very cheerful display, suitable for borders, small beds, pots or rock gardens. The plants are tough and adaptable, growing well in full sun or partial shade. Old plants lose their vigour after the third or fourth year. They should be replaced by new plants which are simple to raise from cuttings taken at any time of the year. They root readily in ordinary garden soil. The mature plants also self-seed and dozens of tiny seedlings are usually to be found in the surrounding ground. These can be dug up and raised anew with no trouble. Young plants should have their growing tips pinched out to produce compact growth. Mature plants should be pruned hard twice a year, in early spring and late summer.

Cigar flower (火絲萼距花, *C. ignea*) has a generally similar appearance to *C. hyssopifolia* except that the flowers are long red tubes with a white tip—resembling a cigar with ash at its tip. Cultivation is the same as with *C. hyssopifolia*.

Custard apple (anona, sugar apple) 番鬼荔枝

Anona squamosa

A small deciduous tree, popular in private gardens where it is grown for its delicious, exotic fruit. The fruit, about the size of a large orange, is green with a scale-like nodular surface, resembling a hand grenade. Inside, numerous shiny black seeds are enclosed in a soft, sweet pulp with an exquisite flavour. The tree grows in full sun or part shade. Smaller specimens, grown in a dragon urn, will fruit well for many years. Container-grown trees will require occasional pruning to restrict size.

Dahlia 楊芍藥
Dahlia sp.

It is only possible to give a general description of the raising of dahlias. These beautiful flowers come in many forms, colours and sizes and the plants may be 30 cm or 1 m high. It is mostly grown in pots and is another important flower in the Chinese New Year season. Dahlias are tuberous rooted and the tubers may be put in during August or September. Staking is usually necessary for the taller varieties. For the less experienced grower, dahlias grown from seed is a less demanding task. Seed-grown dahlias do not come true to parent type. Dwarf varieties with compact, multi-coloured blooms are available. Seeds should be sown in September or October. Cuttings taken in spring root readily and do come true to type. A sunny sheltered position, good drainage and feeding every four weeks are essential.

Daisy (English daisy, common daisy) 春白菊
Bellis perennis

This is the little white flower with the yellow centre that springs up in lawns in temperate climates and is one of the best-loved of European wildflowers. *Bellis* is from the Latin "Bellus" meaning pretty, while daisy is the English corruption of "day's eye", a reference to the flower's tendency to close in the evening and to open to greet the sun in the morning. It is a low shrubby plant with 2.5-cm flowers that consist of white ray-like florets surrounding a yellow disc. This is a cool weather plant that can be easily grown in Hong Kong and should be sown in autumn. Numerous cultivars have produced variations in colour, double flowers and other features, but the white original has the most charm.

Dianthus 石竹屬
Dianthus sp.

A genus of annuals and perennials which includes the carnations, pinks and sweet williams. All are very attractive, scented, and last well as cut flowers. Many varieties can be grown here, but the tall, double-flowered carnations *Dianthus caryophyllus* (麝香石竹 / 丁香花 / 康乃馨) of the florists' variety are a bit difficult for the beginner. While excellent for cutting, it is perhaps less attractive than the more compact and easily raised pinks or *D. chinensis* when grown in beds or pots. Sweet william (*D. barbatus* 十樣竹) can also be grown, and while it is a perennial it is treated as an annual in Hong Kong.

Sow from September to November in pans. Prick out the seedlings to nursery boxes and then to an open nursery bed or to the flowering pot. Soil should be rich and well drained. Avoid excessive watering.

Dieffenbachia (dumb cane) 花葉萬年青

Dieffenbachia picta

This evergreen foliage plant is very suitable for growing indoors or in open shade. It is grown for its large, striking leaves, variegated in green and white or cream. Various cultivars provide many degrees of variegation. It is extremely popular in Hong Kong as it is both attractive and easy to grow. If grown indoors, adequate light from a nearby window is essential. Avoid draughts. Turn the pot occasionally to expose all parts of the plant to the light. Plants have their main growth period in summer and become tall and leggy as winter approaches. They should be replaced each year. Cut off the growing tip with 10 cm of stem and insert in a mixture of sand and peat. The rest of the stem can be cut into 7-cm sections and used as stem cuttings. These cuttings should be inserted so that the tip is just buried in the rooting medium. Otherwise lay the cutting sideways on the surface with a node in contact with the soil. All manner of cuttings succeed easily. The plant is poisonous and is said to produce a severe swelling of the mouth and tongue making speech impossible: hence, "dumb cane".

Dracaena 龍血樹屬

This genus of about 40 shrubby evergreens is grown for their ornamental foliage. At first glance, some dracaenas look so different from one another that it seems they could not possibly be related. Some are tall and willowy, some squat and shrubby. The leaves vary in length, breadth and colour. However, on closer examination, they will all be found to be naturally erect, single-stemmed, with long, sword-shaped leaves gracefully arching out in palm-like fashion. They are usually grown as house plants and need minimal care.

Dracaena fragrans

Dracaena fragrans (巴西鐵樹) is seen everywhere—it is possibly the most popular house plant in Chinese homes. Its Chinese name is "iron tree", and it lives up to its name with its toughness. It is easily obtainable all over Hong Kong—in nurseries, flower stalls and even offered on sidewalks by itinerant peddlers. It is sold looking like a simple log of wood, looking lifeless except for the fresh green shoots sprouting miraculously in several places. The "log" is brought home, placed in a decorative dish with 1 cm of water, and left to get on with the job, which it does with no help from anyone. Its leaves are long-lasting, strap-shaped, mid-dark green, curving gracefully. It is quite happy to spend its entire life indoors. After some years, if the wood begins to rot or the bark to shed, pot it in earth and it will carry on happily. It is, of course, possible to grow it as a pot plant from the very start.

D. sanderiana (辛氏龍樹) is a good-looking small shrub with grey-green leaves. Some varieties have silvery or ivory margins. As cut foliage, this dracaena will last six months in a vase of water, developing roots all the while. It is only necessary to change the water once a week. The rooted stems can be used for propagation by planting in soil.

Very similar in appearance to *D. sanderiana* is *D. reflexa variegata* (分枝鐵樹). However, whereas the former tends to grow straight up with little branching, the latter species throws out branches, producing the appearance of a bushy shrub or a small tree. I first saw a specimen in a friend's garden in Bangkok, and was hugely impressed by its beautiful common name—"Song of India". It is worth growing it for that name alone! The lance-shaped leaves, about 2 cm wide and 20 cm long, grow in compact clusters, in medium green with cream-coloured margins.

D. deremensis or Japanese Dracaena (日本鐵樹) is a shrub or small tree either with all-green leaves or striped with white or silver.

D. marginata (紅邊鐵樹) has tall graceful stems and long leaves edged with red. The leaves are borne at the end of the stems in attractive palm-like fashion. It is a very striking indoor plant. Many cultivars exist, with interesting colour variations.

All dracaenas are easily raised from tip or stem cuttings or from basal shoots.

Dracaena: Song of India

E

Eggplant (aubergine, brinjal) 矮瓜
Solanum melongena

Eggplant is a wonderful warm or cool season vegetable and a beautiful one as well. A relative of the potato and tomato, it is a small shrub about 60 cm tall with lobed leaves. The pendulous fruit are a magnificent rich purple. I never fail to marvel at this colour, especially in the young fruit, when there may be several shades of purple. Grow in summer, sowing the seeds from April to July. The seeds are very similar to those of capsicum and may take up to two weeks to germinate. Place four seeds in a small 5-cm pot and when the seedlings have put out their second leaf, thin out to leave the strongest plant. When it outgrows the pot, transplant into the ground or into a 21-cm pot. Pick the fruit young, when they feel slightly springy and about 12 cm long, and certainly before seeds develop. An autumn sowing in September or October is also possible. Eggplant is available in a variety of shapes—round, egg-shaped, flat, etc., but I like the long purple one best.

Endive 菊苣
Cichorium endiva

(See *Cichorium*, under "Lettuce")

Ferns 芒

Ferns are foliage plants which are unique in that they are neuter plants, producing neither flowers nor seeds. Instead, they reproduce by means of spores. These reproducing spores are carried by the millions on the under surface of the fronds. They are contained in capsules which rupture when ripe, scattering a dust-cloud of spores. Raising plants from spores is an interesting exercise though it may be some time before recognisable plants appear.

There are about ten thousand varieties of ferns all over the world, but mostly in the tropics. It is these tropical ferns that are of the greatest use as cultivated plants. With such a large number of ferns it goes without saying that the varieties of form and habit are enormous. Ferns are common pioneer plants, that is to say, in areas devastated by forest fires, or volcanic eruptions, ferns are among the first new life forms to appear in these situations.

The fronds and roots of most ferns grow from fleshy storage stems or rhizomes which usually spread horizontally under the soil surface. Some, however, take the form of short, branching stems. The fronds are a combination of stalk and blade-like leaf. The shape and size of a frond varies greatly from a simple strap shape to intricate divisions to give it a feathery or lacy appearance.

Certain ferns reproduce not only by spores but by throwing out miniature plantlets or offsets. They can be detached and used for propagation. In practice, cultivated ferns are most usually propagated by division. Ferns need shady, sheltered positions, making them ideally suited for indoor culture. Open shade is ideal for most, but some dappled, early morning sun is beneficial for encouraging growth. Some, especially the wild ferns, tolerate deep shade.

Ferns grow best in a light, slightly acid soil rich in humus or peat. The water requirement is high due to loss of moisture from the fronds, so the soil must always be kept moist though not sodden. Frequent spraying with a fine mist is also helpful.

Maidenhair fern 鐵線蕨
Adiantum capillus-veneris

Maidenhair fern

A popular variety so named because its slender, shiny, black leaf-stalks resemble human hair: the species name actually means "Venus' hair". The graceful fronds are 30–60 cm long and are divided into many roughly triangular, slightly lobed leaflets. New plants can be raised by cutting off sections of the rhizome with one or two fronds attached. Alternatively, divide the whole plant into a number of clumps to be separately potted. Raising from spores is also possible. In the wild, maidenhair fern is often found in lime-rich areas, so some growers recommend the addition of lime to the potting soil.

Bird's nest fern 雀巢芒

Asplenium nidus

So called because its shiny lance-shaped, undivided fronds spread, rosette-fashion, from a central fibrous core, thus resembling a bird's nest. No offsets are produced and propagation is by spores.

Bird's nest fern: spores

Sword fern

Perhaps the most popular and common of the cultivated ferns. There are two popular varieties, both especially suited for hanging baskets.

Nephrolepis cordifolia (腎蕨) produces fairly stiff mid-green fronds up to 1 m long, narrowly pinnate. It is very easy to grow and spreads rapidly by producing numerous stolons on which new offsets appear. These can be snipped off and grown on as new plants. It may also be propagated by the division of the rhizome which often bears tubers.

N. exaltata (毛葉腎蕨) is more widely known as the ever-popular Boston fern. The fronds are similar to *N. cordifolia* but each pinna is itself finely divided to produce a lacy appearance. The elegance of the plant varies according to the delicacy of the feathery fronds. Sometimes a poorly segmented frond appears in the midst of a delicate plant. This should be removed, as left unattended, the plant may revert to the more primitive type. Propagation is similar to *N. cordifolia*.

Nephrolepis is frequently attacked by caterpillars, which should be picked out individually. Their natural camouflage sometimes makes this difficult. Look out for their droppings which betray their presence. *Nephrolepsis* is used in traditional medicine as an anti-pyretic, against inflammation, and as a diuretic.

Numerous other ferns can be successfully grown in Hong Kong but will not be individually described. These include *Blechnum, Davallia, Platycerium, Polypodium, Pteris* and many others.

Sword fern: Nephrolepis cordifolia

Ficus

This huge genus comprises about 800 species in tropical and subtropical regions of the world. They include trees, shrubs, creepers and climbers of very great variety.

The ficus tree most typically associated with Hong Kong is the **small-leaved banyan**, also known as the **Chinese banyan** (榕樹, *Ficus microcarpa*). This is a tree of substantial dimensions, with dense foliage of glossy, leathery, rich-green leaves. The general appearance of the tree remains more or less unchanged throughout the year. Its imposing appearance is largely due to its gnarled and sinewed trunk which gives it immense character. Nathan Road was once a grand avenue, lined on both sides by these magnificent and majestic sentinels, witnesses to our unfolding history. Its fruit are small pea-sized figs, an important source of food for wildlife, especially birds. These birds help to propagate the banyan far and wide. All parts of the tree contain a sticky latex, a feature common to all ficus species.

One of the most prominent features of the tree is the production of aerial roots from its branches, growing downwards, searching for any decent patch of ground from which to draw nutrients and for new growth to spring forth. This accounts for the strange and wonderful phenomenon of banyans growing in the most unlikely situations, such as blank cement or stone walls, with hardly a crack for a foothold, and yet reaching substantial proportions. Scattered around Hong Kong there are many of these old stone walls hosting banyans of great size and age. The most magnificent of these is in Forbes Street (科士街) in Kennedy Town where there is a stone wall over a hundred metres in length, covered with a network of banyan roots. Some of these trees are a hundred years old. So special is this wall that there are plans afoot to have it declared a heritage site. I urge you to visit Forbes Street and have a look for yourself. Sadly many similar stone walls have met their demise with the hunger for land and development. The wide-ranging aerial roots seek out every source of nutrient, even to the extent of enveloping neighbouring trees, and sometimes its own trunk. This phenomenon is known as "strangling", the botanical equivalent of a hostile takeover in the business world. Strangling may become established in another way. Occasionally figs dropped by birds become lodged in branches of other trees or bushes and grow into little banyans. They can develop quite rapidly into substantial plants and in time, may take over completely from the unfortunate host.

Many old banyans at strategic sites are greatly revered by rural communities. In some parts of South Asia a single tree may cover an area of an acre or more. The tree would serve as a focal point for the village, for communal activities, or simply as a place to meet socially.

The **large-leaved banyan** (大葉榕, *F. virens*) is a deciduous tree of considerable size. Perhaps the most attractive time of its cycle is around March, when the sudden appearance of bright, pale-green new leaves announces the arrival of spring. These new leaves are covered by soft, rather elastic stipules that fall off as the leaves emerge, covering the ground around the tree. This stipule, together with the latex contained within all parts of the tree, are twin diagnostic features of all ficus species. The leaves are quite large, up to 12 x 9 cm, of a pleasing mid-green colour, darkening as the season progresses. With its large size and spreading crown, it is a wonderful shade tree. No aerial roots are produced. One particularly fine specimen stands in Garden Road between the Helena May Institute and St. Joseph's Church.

Another common ficus species is the **common red-stemmed fig** (青果榕, *F. variegata*) which grows wild and is widespread in Hong Kong. It exhibits the curious phenomenon of "cauliflory", i.e., the growth of fruit (or flowers) directly from the trunk of the tree, or "ramiflory" if they arise from the branches. Other examples that exhibit cauliflory are the

Common red-stemmed fig

Bo tree

papaya and the jackfruit. Just outside my garden fence stands a 20-m specimen of this tree, providing me with the most wonderful shade. Its spreading, benevolent crown harbours all forms of birdlife (with accompanying birdsong)—warblers, bulbuls, magpie robins, crested mynahs, sparrows, doves and others, all of whom feed on its bounteous fruit. The welcome appearance of an occasional squirrel reminds me that these industrious creatures have not yet died out in Hong Kong. At night, bats flit about and take their turn at the buffet. Inside the fig itself is found a large number of long-tailed fig wasps, a tiny insect that spends the most important parts of its life cycle within the fig itself. This tree sheds its leaves twice a year and, amazingly, the new leaves repopulate its branches in a space of about 10 days even before the last of the old leaves have fallen.

Less common than the above three, but not at all unusual, is the **bo** or **peepul tree** (菩提樹, *F. religiosa*) which grows wild but deserves to be cultivated and used for parks and roadsides. Its heart-shaped leaves draw out to a fine long point making the tree easily recognisable. Siddhartha Gautama, the Buddha, attained enlightenment under the shade of such a tree in Maghada, which is why it is also known as the **tree of enlightenment.** A small specimen grown in a dragon urn is very suitable for a sunny balcony.

The evergreen **weeping fig** (垂葉榕, *F. benjamina*) has, as its name suggests, a slightly weeping habit, with branches drooping at the tips. Otherwise it very much resembles the small-leaved banyan except that its leaves are slightly wavy at the edges and come to a finer point. Its growth habit is more regular, and this more predictable habit makes it suitable for containers and indoor culture. It is the ficus of living rooms, halls and lobbies. It is especially suitable for this role as it grows quite happily in bright shade or limited sunlight. Cultivars with variegated leaves are also available. *F. benjamina* has proved to be one of the most popular trees for urban planting in recent years.

The **edible fig** (無花果, *F. carica*) is indigenous to Turkey but does reasonably well in Hong Kong. It is a small deciduous tree fruiting twice a year. Fresh figs are hardly ever seen in the marketplace, so why not grow your own? The flowers are confined within the fleshy fruit and are therefore not seen. This accounts for its Chinese name of "fruit without flowers". The leaves are distinctively three-lobed, large enough to be used by Adam and Eve to preserve their modesty. It is not necessary to confine the roots as recommended in temperate climates. Nevertheless, the fig does well in a large container such as a dragon urn. Its roots are shallow, so avoid excessive cultivation of the surface soil. Propagation is quite easy, either by air layering or 12-cm heel cuttings. The main crop ripens in the late summer when the figs change

F

from green to a reddish-brown and droop slightly at the stalk. Pick them when dead ripe, when they are just about to split. Birds often beat you to the fruit unless some form of protection is used: netting, or plastic bags. In February, prune lightly to shape the tree and to remove crossing and weak branches.

A delicious syrup can be prepared from fig leaves—a refreshing summer drink very soothing to the throat. For many years this syrup used to be available for sale in small quantities at the Carmelite Convent in Stanley. The sisters have a number of trees in their quadrangle for a good supply of fig leaves.

Fig syrup 無花果甘露

Ingredients

- 40 fresh fig leaves
- 3 kg rock or golden brown sugar
- White and shell of one egg
- 6 L water

Method

- Boil the leaves in the water for one hour.
- Remove the leaves, then add the rock sugar and simmer until completely dissolved. Sieve the liquid, then add the white of one egg together with the egg shell. Continue to simmer for five hours.
- A light scum that forms on the surface will adhere to the egg white and shell, and can be conveniently scooped away as it forms.
- The finished product is a deep golden-brown and has the consistency of honey. Try it!

The **Indian rubber tree** (印度榕, *F. elastica*) is well distributed in Hong Kong, growing to a large size in the wild or in cultivation. It is characterised by large, thick, leathery leaves 20 cm long with a prominent midrib. It also produces numerous aerial roots. It may not be a good choice for home gardens as its root structure is very invasive and tends to discourage other plants around it. Small specimens are favourite house plants: the ubiquitous rubber plant grown in containers for its attractive leaves which can be polished to a high shine. Cultivars include "Decora" with bronze-coloured new leaves and "Doescheri" with variegated grey-green leaves with cream highlights and a pink midrib. These plants are easily raised by air-layering. With its high rate of success, the rubber plant is a good introduction to the air-layering technique. Plants that grow too large should be discarded and replaced by new young ones.

Creeping fig

It is difficult to believe that the large trees described above are relatives of the **creeping fig** (薜荔, *F. pumila*), which is only a humble creeper. It grows slowly but relentlessly up any surface by means of aerial roots along the stems. This plant makes a good evergreen wall-covering and its small, slightly heart-shaped leaves will soften an ugly pillar, rough plaster wall or any other surface that needs a green cover. It is very simply raised from cuttings. I am pleased to see this plant covering the concrete buttresses of some of our ugly road flyovers.

Firecracker vine 炮仗花
Pyrostegia ignea

A most attractive climbing vine with dense clusters of orange tubular flowers appearing in December. A native of Central and South America, it has done so well in Hong Kong that it has become one of the most popular of all climbers. In full flower it is one of the most magnificent of all climbing vines. The show lasts about six weeks. The flowers are borne in clusters of 15 to 20, each having a 6–7 cm long corolla tube that opens up trumpet-like. The plant derives its name from the fact that the unopened flowers, when stamped underfoot, give off a popping sound, much like an exploding firecracker. The bunched flowers also look like strings of firecrackers.

The base of the flower tube contains a pleasant sweet-tasting nectar. This delight can be sampled by pulling out a fully-opened flower and sucking the nectar from the base of the tube. Although it can be raised from cuttings, these are not routinely successful and it is more convenient to purchase a young plant from a nursery. A lot of growth is made in a year and it is therefore useful if rapid cover is required. It does, however, require good support such as a fence or open wall, and is not suitable for smooth walls or slopes. The plant thrives in local conditions and tolerates any soil as long as it receives full sun. No pruning or any special care is required.

Fukien tea 福建茶樹
Carmona microphylla

This small-to-medium shrub is grown for its densely packed, shiny green leaves, each about 1.5 cm long and slightly lobulated. Its dense habit and tolerance of repeated pruning make it a good low hedge. Fukien tea is a popular and affordable bonsai plant, and can be pruned to artistic and exotic formations. Small, white, star-shaped flowers are produced in summer but are of little attraction when compared to its foliage.

Gaillardia (blanket flower) 天人菊
Gaillardia

This genus of annuals, biennials and perennials are all native to the United States. They are treated locally as annuals started from seed in autumn. The flowers are daisylike, single or double. The common name of "blanket flower" arose because the rich yellow, red, and orange colours are reminiscent of the colours found in the traditional blankets used by the native Americans. It grows in any soil provided there is full sun. The flowers are good for cutting.

Geranium 天竺葵屬
Pelargonium sp.

The common or garden geranium is a zonal pelargonium, and should not be confused with the genus *Geranium*. This small perennial shrub is distinguished by its rounded mid-green leaves with a conspicuous brownish-reddish zone. The flowers are five-petalled, the two upper petals often being larger. They are borne in rounded umbels in scarlet, pink or white. Numerous hybrids provide a dazzling array of colours and forms. Mostly pot-grown, the geranium is also the quintessential window box ornamental.

Start the plants in October, using 7 cm cuttings rooted in an equal mixture of peat moss and sand. A number of seed strains are now available and should be sown in autumn. Keep the young plants in a sunny position. They are not much good in shade. In the early stages of growth, pinch off the growing tips to shape and expand the plant sideways. Feed every two weeks. Remove the flowers after they fade as this stimulates new growth. At the end of the flowering season, cut back the plant by one third to one half. This is not necessary, however, if taller or more dramatic branching is desired. Geraniums give forth their best blooms when somewhat pot-bound. Generally they should be re-potted every other year, and when doing so, use only a slightly larger pot.

An interesting group of *Pelargoniums* is the collection of **scented-leafed hybrids**. Most are dense shrubs with lobed or deeply dissected leaves that are often hairy. The range of scented essential oils in the leaves is very wide, the scents ranging through peppermint, lemon, apple, rose and even coconut. The most strongly scented of these is the lemon. Flowers are usually small and not very prominent.

Gerbera (African daisy) 非洲菊
Gerbera jamesonii

A perennial flowering plant producing daisy-like flowers during the summer months. The colours are very varied, coming in shades of red, orange, pink or cream. The leaves are prominently lobed and arranged in rosettes. African daisy is highly prized as a cut flower, but as a garden ornamental it is not particularly effective as out of flower it looks a bit ragged. A deep-rooting plant, it is not suitable for containers.

Ginger lily 薑花

Hedychium coronarium

This native of India is one of many herbaceous perennials with stems arising in clumps from rhizomes. The exotic, pure-white flowers have a satiny texture and are borne in loose clusters from August to December. The long, lanceolate leaves are slightly downy underneath. A commercially important flower, it is valued as a cut flower because of its heady perfume that will fill any room. It looks a little untidy when out of flower and may not be suitable for a small garden. Propagation is by division of the rhizome.

Globe amaranth 千日紅

Gomphrena globosa

The globe amaranth is an old, reliable friend, providing a colourful display in the late summer and early autumn. The flowers are elongated globes with a spongy appearance and a papery texture, in red and purple. The leaves are hairy and opposite. They are mostly seen as pot plants but are equally effective in small or large beds. For everlasting flowers, cut the flowers just before they reach maturity and hang them upside down in a cool airy place, but not in the sun. The dried flowers come in handy for winter floral arrangements.

Raise *Gomphrena* from seed sown between March and May. The young plants should be pinched back from time to time to encourage a bushy habit and more flowers. Grow in a sunny site.

Gloxinia 大岩桐 / 洛仙花

Sinningia speciosa

This striking flowering plant is particularly useful for Hong Kong because it prefers shade and can therefore be raised in any verandah or window sill. It is perfect for pot culture. The very tiny seeds should be mixed with fine sand and sown in pans in October. Scatter the seeds on the surface of fine soil and gently tamp them in with a flat board. They germinate readily. Prick out the seedlings singly into small plastic pots and transplant as soon as they are established. In spring, showy velvety bell-shaped flowers with short rounded lobes at the mouth are produced in many rich colours, usually with a dark throat, often white-rimmed or variegated. Watering should be directly onto the soil which should be kept just moist and not soggy.

Golden candles 黃鴨嘴花
Pachystachus lutea

A cheerful display of golden yellow "candles" rising up from a low-growing shrub is what makes this plant unusual. The "candles"' are made up of colourful bracts. Its white flowers emerge from between the bracts, but not until the bracts are fully developed. This is an extremely useful source of colour in the summer months. Propagate from cuttings in February.

Golden dewdrop 假連翹
Duranta repens

This much-branched shrub can grow to a height of 3 m, producing sprays of delicate mauve flowers followed by drooping bunches of golden berries. Mostly, though, it is grown for its always fresh-looking green foliage. As a pot plant or a garden shrub it is often clipped to a dome shape. Each pruning stimulates a new growth of light green leaves. It is an excellent choice for a hedge, a stand-alone shrub or small tree. It does best in a sunny site but is not particular about soil. In spring or summer, take cuttings of the growing tips, about 9 cm long with some of the young wood. They take with ease.

Herbalists have used this plant as an anti-malarial and for promoting the circulation.

Guava 蕃石榴
Psidium guajava

This small tropical evergreen tree of irregular shape grows to 4–5m. Its bark is distinctive, with blotchy areas of various shades of brown and cream, and peels away in patches. Its wood is exceptionally hard and can be used as tools for grinding or pounding. Young boys value catapults made from its wood. The fruit is a round or oval berry, green at first, ripening to a light green or pale yellow. Its delicious flesh is very fragrant, and surrounds hundreds of small seeds packed in the centre. Although not grown commercially in Hong Kong, the fruit is sometimes available in markets. It is also made into juice and a very distinctive-tasting jam.

Guava bark

Heavenly bamboo 南天竹

Nandina domestica

This is a single species from China and Japan. Also known as Chinese sacred bamboo, this is not a bamboo at all. It has a resemblance to bamboo in its cane-like stems, branching lightly, and in its finely textured, delicate foliage. New leaves are red, later turning green. With the approach of colder weather the older leaves develop yellow, crimson and brown tinges, before falling. The plant seems to change its appearance regularly.

Heavenly bamboo thrives in Hong Kong though it is relatively slow growing. It may be used both for ground planting or for pots 21 cm and larger. For a medium-height screen, say 1–1.5 m high, there is no better choice. It has a light, delicate, elegant look, and is very effective with night lighting. It grows best in filtered sun and prefers rich, well-drained soil. It makes a good indoor plant if given enough light. It can easily be propagated in spring or summer from cuttings which have a high strike rate.

Herbs 芳草

Many people grow herbs, even if they grow nothing else. All you need is a balcony or just a windowsill, and you can grow useful herbs for the kitchen. Though I have seen many different herbs being grown in Hong Kong, I shall describe only those that I have tried successfully.

Basil (九層塔, *Ocimum basilicum*) is deservedly many people's favourite "western" herb. Actually it is native to the tropical areas of Africa, Asia and the Middle East. Basil is steeped in religious history, and is believed to be an abbreviated form of *Basilikon photon*, or "kingly herb" in Greek. It is said to have grown around the tomb of Jesus after the resurrection.

It grows readily from seed and can be kept going throughout the year. One or two plants in 10-cm pots will keep you in good supply for several months. It needs at least four hours of sunshine a day and good drainage. Pinch out the growing tips in order to keep the plant bushy and productive. If grown in the ground, sow the seeds directly where they are to grow. Ground-grown bushes can be quite large—about 40 cm or so high. Keep a few flowering spikes to produce seeds which can be saved for the next season. Replace the shrub after two years or simply treat it as an annual.

Apart from sweet basil, there are many cultivars selected for their fragrance, flavour and colour. So-called "Thai basil" covers at least eight plants, different in subtle ways. Generally, Thai basil has a stronger flavour, with a suggestion of cloves.

I have also grown Greek basil (var. Minimum) from seed which I collected on a trip to Israel. It is used in the Greek Orthodox Church for sprinkling holy water. This is a more compact plant, very suitable for window boxes. It has smaller leaves and grows to about 20 cm in height. All types of basil are easy to grow.

Those of us who grow basil know that store-bought dried basil leaves are a pale reflection of the fresh product. Excess basil leaves can be gathered to make your own fresh pesto, which by itself is a good enough reason for growing it. A simple pesto recipe follows.

Pesto sauce 香草醬

Ingredients

- 4 cups chopped fresh basil leaves
- 4 cloves crushed garlic
- 1 cup pine nuts (or walnuts)
- 1 cup grated Parmesan cheese
- 1 1/2 cups extra virgin olive oil
- Salt and pepper

Method

- Lightly toast the pine nuts in a non-stick pan until a light brown.
- Put the pine nuts, chopped basil leaves, cheese and garlic in a blender and blend at a low speed, adding the olive oil slowly. The actual amount of olive oil used can be varied according to the consistency desired.
- Add salt and pepper to taste.
- Serve fresh with pasta, grilled chicken or fish, or use as a dip. Any remainder can be kept in a refrigerator for a week. Don't bother to freeze: make a new batch instead.

Bay leaves (月桂, *Laurus nobilis*) come from the bay laurel, also known as the bay tree or sweet laurel. In history, a "crown of laurels" was fashioned from the branches of this dense shrub or small tree as a mark of excellence for athletes and poets. In Hong Kong it is usually grown in pots, but I have seen quite large shrubs up to 2 m tall in some old gardens. Today it is grown for its leaves which are used as a culinary herb for its spicy fragrance. Fresh bay leaves are vastly superior to the dried variety. It is also useful as an ornamental shrub and can be trained as a standard. It is prone to infestation by scale. Discard the heavily infested leaves or scrape off the scale from the under surfaces of the leaves. Propagation is by heel cuttings but the strike rate is quite unpredictable.

Chinese chives (韭菜, *Allium tuberosum*) are easily grown from seed, from April through to September. They have flat, narrow, dark green leaves. A blanched variety is also marketed, and is produced commercially by covering the young plants with special pots or "chimneys" to cut out the sun. The home gardener can achieve a similar effect by simply covering the plants with an inverted flower pot. The flowering stem, with the flower in bud form, is also a popular vegetable in wet markets.

Chinese chives

Coriander (芫荽, *Coriandrum sativum*), also known as Chinese parsley, is perhaps my personal favourite "local" herb, used in a vast variety of dishes. Sow the seeds from September to April. The seeds are large and hard, and may take quite a while to germinate—10 days or more. Soaking the seeds in water for a few hours may hasten germination. If you sow in pots every four weeks or so, you can keep up a succession to last throughout the season which is from October to May. Coriander is difficult to maintain in high summer. Although usually sold as a whole plant, roots and all, the leaves can be picked instead, thereby prolonging the production period. The crushed, dry seed is also an important ingredient in Asian cooking.

Coriander

Curry leaves (調料九里香 / 咖哩葉, *Murraya koenigi*) may not be familiar to everyone, but in south Asian cooking it is a highly sought-after ingredient. The English word *curry* is derived from the Tamil word *kari* which means a "sauce". Allied to citrus, the plant is an evergreen shrub or small tree with creamy white flowers and pinnate leaves with about 10 pairs of leaves. The leaves are highly aromatic, and are used for curries and stews. The fruits are small, black and berry-like, enclosing a seed from which it can be propagated. It may also be grown from basal offshoots or propagated by cuttings. It benefits from a light pruning from time to time to limit its size and to keep its shape. (See curry recipe under "Okra".)

Curry leaves

Galangal (砂薑, *Kaempferia galangal* syn. *Alpinia officianarum*) is another spice important to Asian cuisine, especially Thai, Malaysian and Indian cuisine. The plant is grown for its rhizomes which have a taste that resembles ginger. The leaves appear tightly furled, then open to an almost round shape with a pointed tip. Venation is parallel or almost so. It can be grown from pieces of the rhizome obtained from spice shops. One plant grown in a pot should be sufficient for home use. It may die down in winter to re-emerge in the spring. In Chinese grocery shops it is usually sold in the dried powdered form, especially good for flavouring steamed chicken. It is also a herbal remedy used by traditional medicine practitioners for a host of complaints.

Galangal

Ginger (薑, *Zingiber officinale*), together with spring onions, is essential in Chinese cuisine, especially in steamed dishes such as fish. Grow ginger from any rhizome obtained from the market. It needs little care but the soil must be sandy and loose, otherwise only very small rhizomes will result. Ginger is used medicinally as an effective carminative, to settle the stomach and to relieve "wind".

Lemon grass (香茅, *Cymbogon citratus*) has become hugely popular, in line with the rising interest in Thai food. The plant looks like a very coarse erect grass with the stalks forming clumps above the soil. The simplest way to raise a plant is to obtain a fresh stalk (with some roots attached) from the market and simply stick it in the soil. My plants are all grown in pots. They need little attention, and indeed spread quite rapidly. Grow new plants by division of the clumps. This herb is available year-round, although it does best in summer. Medicinally, lemon grass is used to treat fevers, diarrhoea and menstrual problems. Pure lemon grass essential oil is used in India to treat ringworm and fungal skin infections.

Parsley (洋芫荽, *Petroselinum crispum*) is best grown in cool weather. Italian flat parsley (*P. crispum* var. neapolitanum) also succeeds admirably and grows rapidly. Both these types can be grown in succession in small 10-cm pots to keep up a constant supply.

Rosemary (迷迭香, *Rosmarinus officinalis*) is a small shrubby plant that is also quite ornamental. It does best in poor soil with good drainage, in a sunny site. My ground-grown specimens all fell victim to drowning by heavy rains in the summer, so I suggest they should be grown in pots which can be taken to shelter in rainstorms.

Spring onions (蔥, *Allium cepa*) is certainly the most important local herb. A few sprigs are usually handed out free as a bonus when you purchase other vegetables in a wet market. It can be grown from seeds from September to November but it can be more easily started from its bulbs (shallots). An even simpler way to keep up a small home supply—simply cut off the lower 5 cm of the fleshy stem, roots attached, and plant directly into a small pot. Growth is very rapid and the tops can be cut for use as required in two or three weeks.

Turmeric (黃薑粉, *Curcuma longa*) is a rhizomatous plant of the ginger family and is grown in much the same way as ginger.

Lemon grass

Italian parsley

Mint

You must, however, find yourself a piece of root, which is difficult but not impossible. Turmeric is usually sold as the powdered product, a rich orange-yellow colour, used for flavouring and colouring. It is a cheap alternative to the very expensive saffron. An extract of turmeric, curcumin, is used both in traditional and western medicine. There is good evidence it is a powerful anti-oxidant. It also is known to have some anticancer properties, and partially inhibits the HIV virus. Latest research, published in a prestigious medical journal, shows it is very effective in preventing vascular dysfunction.

Other herbs that can be raised with success are **mint, fennel, garlic, dill** and **arugula.**

Hibiscus

Hibiscus sp.

The mention of hibiscus conjures up the innumerable cultivars of *Hibiscus rosa-sinensis.* In reality, the genus is extremely diverse, with more than 200 species.

Chinese hibiscus

Hibiscus 'Surfrider'

Hibiscus 'Cooperi'

The **Chinese hibiscus** (大紅花, *H. rosa-sinensis*) is an evergreen shrub or small tree, widely and easily grown in Hong Kong. Its leaves are dark green, ovate, coarsely toothed and with pointed tips. The flowers are large, about 12 cm across, with a central column of fused stamens, and are borne singly in the upper leaf axils. The simplest single-petal red hibiscus remains my favourite of this group. However, some of the newer cultivars and hybrids can take your breath away with their large blooms and exotic colours. One example is 'Surfrider' with huge, 15-cm blooms of rich yellow with a dark-red heart. New blooms appear every day. I have a large container-grown specimen in my verandah. A newly-opened flower in the early morning is so striking in appearance that I cannot simply pass one by without saying: "Good Morning, how are you today?"

The shrubs are vigorous in habit, flowering more or less throughout the year, except perhaps, the two coldest months. It is not too particular with soil and will grow in full sun or partial shade but they are heavy feeders and should be fertilised every two weeks. Shrubs that need their size controlled can be given their first pruning of the year in February. This can be a hard prune, to 10 cm from the ground. Alternatively, the shrub can be pruned repeatedly throughout the spring and summer to keep size and shape under control. If grown as a standard, hibiscus makes a very handsome small tree. Tolerance of frequent pruning makes it possible to use hibiscus as a hedge. An attractive hedge can be made of the cultivar 'Cooperi' which has smaller, narrower leaves variegated with cream, crimson and olive. It also has single, red flowers, but when grown as a hedge, the flowers are seldom allowed to develop. The young, woody prunings can be used for cuttings which strike readily. Watch out for aphids and red spider mites.

Fringed hibiscus (吊燈花, *H. schizopetalus*) is a more open, graceful shrub than the Chinese hibiscus. The flowers have delicate, deeply fringed petals, curling sharply backwards. The stamen column protrudes prominently with the stamens clustered at the tip like a miniature feather duster. Its growth habit is similar to the Chinese hibiscus. However, it is not dense enough to grow as a hedge.

Rose of Sharon (木槿, *H. syriacus*) is another widely cultivated variety, mostly with double blooms. It has a wider colour range—red, orange, yellow, mauve and others. A very attractive shrub for private gardens or parks.

The so-called **sleeping hibiscus** or **Turk's cap** (垂花懸鈴花, *Malaviscus arboreus*) is so named because the red, pendulous flowers never seem to open. Some shrubs have pink flowers. It is quick growing and mostly used as a hedge because of its dense foliage. However, its leaves seem to yellow quite easily which detracts slightly from its appearance.

Hollyhock 蜀葵

Althea rosea

This statuesque, very attractive plant may reach heights of 2 m or more. Although a biennial, it is grown as an annual in Hong Kong. As an annual it will reach about 1.5 m in height. The large flowers, single or double, are produced in succession on tall spikes, making it a very suitable background plant. It can also be grown in large 30-cm pots. The leaves are light green and hairy with five or six lobes.

The large, flat seeds should be sown directly in the pot in October. Plant four seeds to a pot and later thin out to leave the strongest seedling standing. Grow in a sunny position out of strong wind. Staking with a stout bamboo is required.

Honeysuckle 金銀花

Lonicera japonica

A spring flowering evergreen twining climber, very popular in Hong Kong. The paired, tubular flowers are white at first, ageing to a pale yellow as the petals open and curl back. Its sweet nectar is a magnet to visiting bees and birds. The flowers have an exquisite, subtle fragrance, most noticeable at night. The dried flowers may be used to prepare a pleasant herbal tea-like drink. It has also been used since the Tang dynasty as a medication which is said to clear the blood.

Honeysuckle can be started by cuttings of the semimature wood anytime in summer. Young plants are also readily available in nurseries. Grow against good support—an open wire fence, trellis or pergola. The growing shoots climb rapidly by twining around their support, making rapid progress, and sometimes strangling neighbouring shrubs and trees. The streamers may have to be cut back from time to time to prevent them from spreading excessively. The plant is quite trouble-free and no special care or pruning is required, except for a light trimming after flowering. Honeysuckle remains decorative for its dense, dark green foliage even after the flowering season. It makes an excellent screen.

Honolulu vine (Queen's wreath, coral vine) 珊瑚籐
Antigonon leptopus

A quick-growing perennial vine which thrives in the heat of summer. It is frequently seen growing wild. In autumn, huge sprays of small pink or white flowers cover the whole vine. Each flower is roughly conical in shape, about 1m long. When in flower it is so eye-catching that one wonders why it is not more popular in gardens, especially as it provides useful cut flowers as well. The reason could be that after flowering, the vine tends to look wild and ragged, with leaves drying up among the tangled vines. Easily raised from seed.

Hydrangea 繡球花
Hydrangea macrophylla

Hydrangeas produce large globular clusters of flowers about 15 cm across. A good specimen can be a glorious sight. Nevertheless, it never reaches the spectacular displays one sees in temperate climates. Its leaves are large and rough, with toothed edges. It needs cool, humid conditions and dappled shade. Decent specimens can be found in public gardens on the Peak. It tends to wilt in the hot sun. It likes soil rich in organic content and is a heavy feeder. Flowers, produced in summer, come in various shades of blue and pink. Blue flowering plants produce their best colour when grown in acid soil. Additions of peat moss, iron or aluminium sulphate will aid this end. Pink varieties prefer alkaline conditions and tend to take on a purple hue in acid soil. To preserve the pink colour, treat the soil with powdered lime. In February, prune back to the old wood. The prunings can be used for cuttings.

Hydrangeas make excellent pot plants. In these days of globalisation, most of the hydrangeas you find in shops will have only just arrived by air from Europe or Taiwan a few days earlier. If these plants are to be kept for the next season, they should be re-potted after flowering, replacing the light growing medium with rich loamy garden soil.

Impatiens 鳳仙花科

Impatiens sp.

An indication of the ease of cultivation of this genus is given by its name, which refers to the "impatience" with which these plants grow and spread. This is a very large genus of over 800 succulent-stemmed annuals and perennials spread throughout the tropics and subtropics of Asia and Africa.

Balsam (鳳仙花, *Impatiens balsamina*), together with zinnias and cockscombs, are the most useful annuals for Hong Kong's hot and humid summers. The erect soft-stemmed plants have mid-green lanceolate leaves with flowers appearing in the axils. White, pink, scarlet and purple forms are available, single or double. It is mostly used as a pot plant but is also suitable for beds. Grows well and reliably in Hong Kong, producing a colourful summer show.

Sow the seeds in pans from March through July. Germination occurs in four to seven days. When the second leaves appear, transplant to 21-cm flowering pots, five to a pot, eventually keeping the best three. If they are awaiting transfer to beds they can, if space is not available, first be transplanted singly into small plastic pots. They will be ready for the final transplantation when the roots begin to crowd the pot. Balsams tolerate a good deal of shade and are therefore particularly valuable for verandahs and shady corners. Seeds from the mature plants can be collected for the following season.

The **busy lizzie** (非洲鳳仙, *I. walleriana*) grows better in the cooler months, and competes with the marigold as the quickest way to bring colour into the garden. Masses of flattish, five-petalled, spurred flowers in an ever-increasing colour range—red, orange, blue, white, pink—will light up the garden with colours. Large beds are especially attractive. It will grow in full or part sun. Tip-prune the plants to encourage a bushy habit and to keep its height to within 25 cm. The flowers readily give way to seed pods. These should be removed early, unless seeds need to be saved for the following season. The ripe seed pods burst open quite forcefully if disturbed, spreading the seeds everywhere. Propagation is by seed although cuttings take readily anytime during the growing season.

New Guinea hybrids are increasingly popular and large numbers of these plants are imported into Hong Kong. These hybrids have bronze-green leaves, oval and pointed and stout, succulent stems, with much larger flowers that may be many-layered. They are very good pot plants and can be grown indoors in bright shade.

Ixora, Chinese 龍船花

Ixora chinensis

This is one of a large genus of about 400 species. Some may be found growing wild in the hills. The shrub is many-stemmed with numerous red flowers collected in a disc-shaped head 7–9 cm across. Each tiny flower is a long tube ending in four rounded lobes. Ixora flowers almost throughout the year, except perhaps in the coolest months of December to February. In February it needs a hard prune. It sometimes sets fruit in the form of berries. Propagation is by cuttings though the strike rate is not high.

Chinese ixora

A dwarf species ***Ixora coccinea*** (紅鮮單花) is also cultivated as a free-flowering shrub. The flowers have pointed corolla lobes. Its dense growth makes it an ideal, colourful hedge, and it is in this form that it has become widespread in Hong Kong in recent years. Flowers are orange-red and far more profuse in this dwarf version. Frequent pruning of the hedges encourages its flowering habit, making it very effective in mass planting. A less common yellow variety is also available but the colour is rather dull compared to the orange-red specimens.

Ivy 常春藤

Hedera helix

This climber has a rampant habit in temperate zones, covering walls, arbours and houses with its attractive foliage. In Hong Kong this role is given to Boston ivy instead. *Hedera* is more usually a pot plant which takes advantage of its trailing habit. It can also be trained to grow erect around a support. Its leaves show many forms, but most commonly are three- to five-lobed with a pointed apex. Propagation is by cuttings.

Jacob's ladder (slipper flower, redbird cactus, zigzag plant) 紅雀珊瑚

Pedilanthus tithymaloides

In Genesis 28:12–13 Jacob has a dream of a ladder reaching up to heaven, with angels going up and down. The appearance of this plant, with the aid of a little imagination, is said to bring this ladder to mind.

This succulent slow-growing, bushy shrub is a native of the Caribbean. It is best as a pot plant—a 10–15 cm pot should be large enough. I spotted a lovely specimen some time ago while on a trip to Bali. Like any good gardener, who keeps his eyes open wherever he might be, I hurriedly and surreptitiously took a few cuttings which became the mother of all my "Bali plants". Many of these have found good homes among my favoured friends.

It has long sparsely-branching stems characterised by a zigzag formation, that is, changing growth direction at every node. Therefore it is sometimes known as the zigzag plant. The leaves are stiff, waxy, usually variegated green and white, and often tipped with pink. The foliage and the unusual stem structure are its main attractions. Its small flowers are seldom produced, especially if grown indoors.

It is a good shade plant and does well as a verandah plant. A few hours of sun a day is helpful as excessive confinement in a shady area will lead to leaf drop. If kept indoors, the plant should be taken out for a dose of sunshine every 10 days or so. Keep the roots slightly pot-bound and water sparingly. Pot-grown plants suffer wind damage quite easily and should be taken indoors when strong northeast winter monsoons blow. They also need some protection when temperatures fall below 13°C. Tip cuttings, 7 cm long, should be started in summer. The strike rate is about 50%. The cut ends exude latex and this can be stopped by immersing in water or charcoal. Root in a very sandy rooting medium which should be kept only slightly moist.

Herbalists use this plant as an anti-inflammatory and haemostatic.

Jasmine 素馨屬

Jasminum sp.

Arabian jasmine (茉莉花, *Jasminum sambac*) has pure-white flowers with a clean, penetrating fragrance that is familiar to most people. And who has not enjoyed the subtlety of jasmine tea? Jasmine is grown as an evergreen shrub with a moderately sprawling, irregular habit. Frequent pinching of the growing tips is required to hold back the long streamers which tend to spread in all directions. An untended plant can be very untidy. It grows well in ordinary soil and does equally well in sun or part shade. The flowers, which appear in summer, are white and double, emitting their famous perfume. The cut flowers are often sold in small bunches by hawkers. Propagation is by cuttings in spring or by layering.

Indian or **hairy jasmine** (毛茉莉, *J. multiflorum*) is a woody climber that grows both in full sun and part shade. It is grown to best effect on a trellis, against a wall. It climbs by twining, but some tying down is needed at intervals to direct otherwise errant growth. It can also be grown as a shrub if correctly pruned. Flowers appear in abundance in October and then in smaller displays for two months or so. It has a subtle perfume, best appreciated at night, though less intense than Arabian jasmine. Propagation is by cuttings or by detaching new shoots from the base of established plants. After flowering, thin out the extensive growth made in the previous year though there is no need for a regular pruning.

Yellow or **winter jasmine** (黃素馨, *J. primulinum* syn. *J. mesnyi*) is a very popular and widely grown shrub prized for its graceful appearance. The slender, curving branches make it ideal for growing on a bank. In spring numerous bright yellow flowers, single or double and about 3 cm across, are produced making a very attractive display. There is no scent to this jasmine. Even out of flower the shrub is very decorative. In January, prune lightly, taking care to preserve the long curving branches. Dead wood should also be removed at this time. Propagation is by cuttings of the semi-mature wood which root readily in ordinary garden soil at any time. Established plants propagate themselves by layering, wherever the branches come into contact with the ground. When rooted these new plants can be detached and grown on independently.

Indian jasmine

Jatropha (peregrina, violin-leaved nut) 粉花琴葉珊瑚
Jatropha pandurifolia

This is an extremely useful small flowering tree from the West Indies suitable for small gardens. It has a spreading crown but can be kept to a small size by proper pruning. Its glossy green leaves have a wavy margin reminiscent (with some imagination, I suppose) of the outline of a violin. Throughout the summer, small clusters of red, five-petalled, funnel-shaped flowers are produced at the ends of the branches. The flowers are not profuse but are constantly renewed. The overall effect is very pleasing. Full sun is best but it tolerates part shade. Propagation is possible by cuttings in summer.

Joseph's coat 雁來紅
Amaranthus tricolor

A robust bushy plant grown for its handsome foliage. Sow the seeds in March for a colourful mid-summer display. The lower leaves are usually dull green or bronze leading up to a crown of brilliant crimson foliage. The many cultivated strains range from low bedding plants to bushy annuals up to 1 m tall in a variety of vivid colours. (Also see "Chinese spinach".)

Juniper, Chinese 檜刺柏
Juniperis chinensis

A bushy, cone-shaped evergreen coniferous shrub or tree. A very effective garden ornamental, especially when grown in rows or clumps. Of slow growth, it tolerates almost any kind of soil and is relatively trouble-free. A small specimen in a 30-cm pot will do nicely as a Christmas tree, year after year. After the Christmas season, when divested of streamers and baubles indoors, it is moved back to the garden. A reusable, economical eco-friendly alternative indeed to the poorly shaped local pine or the expensive imported conifers—not to mention the garish artificial trees. Pot-grown plants should be watered moderately. There are many horticultural variations to choose from, such as the dwarf form, with a low spreading habit best for rock gardens, Japanese gardens and so forth.

Kai choi (leaf mustard) 芥菜

Brassica juncea

What makes this vegetable so valuable is that it can be grown in the height of summer when table greens are scarce. In the earlier summer months, grow Chinese spinach or water spinach, and follow these with kai choi. Sow the seeds in July in pans and transplant out when 7 cm high. It grows rapidly and is ready for the table in about eight weeks. A second crop can still be planted before setting out your winter vegetables. My own preference, however, is to extend the useful production of the first crop by picking the outer leaves for use as required instead of pulling the whole plant—the way it usually appears in the markets. Kai choi can also be grown, probably even more successfully, in winter. Watch out for aphids.

Another variety of kai choi is the **Swatow mustard** (大芥菜) which has a well-formed, fleshy heart around a stout stem. This vegetable can be eaten fresh, stir-fried, but is more usually used in a preserved, pickled form. A great home-made crunchy pickle can be made from this vegetable. This is how my ancient amah used to make it:

Swatow mustard pickles 辣菜

Ingredients

- Two swatow mustard hearts
- 500 mL Chinese white vinegar
- 400 g brown or rock sugar
- 4 tsp. Coleman's mustard
- 1 knob ginger, sliced
- 3 hot red chillis

Method

- Trim the swatow mustard hearts by removing the outer leaves.
- Cut into pieces about 5 cm x 5 cm. Wash and lay aside.
- Heat the vinegar, ginger and sugar in a pan over low heat until the sugar is completely dissolved.
- Stir in the mustard and allow to cool.
- Add the swatow mustard pieces and the chillies and transfer to a suitable bottle.
- The pickles should be ready to eat in 48 hours!

Kai lan (Chinese flowering kale) 芥蘭
Brassica alboglabra

A truly delicious winter vegetable and a strong challenger to choi sum as my favourite winter vegetable. Sow in pans, from September through November. Transplant out when 7 cm high, keeping the plants 15 cm apart each way. Feed weekly with a dilute liquid fertiliser. Mature kale has sturdy, erect stalks up to 5 cm across at the base. The leaves are thick and waxy, with a fine bloom. Harvest the vegetable when the white flowers just begin to open, cutting the stem cleanly with a sharp knife. Leave about two or three side shoots to provide a second crop.

Kai lan is best cooked whole in the following way. First soften the vegetable by blanching in boiling water for two or three minutes. Rinse in cold water and drain. Meanwhile, heat some vegetable oil with some crushed ginger. Toss the kai lan in the oil briefly, with a pinch of salt and a sprinkling of sugar. Finally add a tablespoon of Chinese rice wine. Enjoy!

Kalanchoe 紅川蓮
Kalanchoe flammea

This genus comprises many species of perennial succulents varying from low leafy specimens to small shrubs. Kalanchoe is grown for both its ornamental foliage as well as its flowers. In Hong Kong it is usually grown as a pot plant and is in plentiful supply in florist shops where most of the plants are flown in from abroad. *Kalanchoe flammea* grows to about 15 cm high and in winter, dense clusters of flowers provide very vivid colour. Orange, yellow and red forms are the most common. Propagate by cuttings.

Kohlrabi 芥蘭頭

Brassica oleracea var. Caulorapa

This is a vegetable that deserves far more attention. It is a biennial grown as an annual. It is grown for its light green, swollen globular stem which appears just above the ground and which resembles a leafy turnip. There the resemblance ends because kohlrabi is far superior in flavour and texture. A purple variety is also available. A winter vegetable, it can be sown from October through December. Like the turnip, it can be used as a catch crop towards the end of the winter vegetable season. Sow the seeds in the ground 1 cm deep, 15 cm apart each way. Put three seeds in each drill and later thin out to retain the strongest seedling to grow to maturity undisturbed. Seeds may also be sown in pans or small plastic pots for later transplantation when the seedlings are 7 cm high. As the stem swells it lifts itself off ground level, and care should be taken to build up soil around it from time to time. Pick off the lower leaves regularly. It is important not to let the plants grow old as the texture then becomes quite fibrous. Harvest when still tender—about the size of a small orange. Raw kohlrabi, cut in small strips, adds a very pleasant crunch to any salad. It may also be successfully grown in pots, one plant to a 21-cm pot.

Kumquat 金橘屬

Fortunella sp.

These bright, orange fruits come in two versions, oval-shaped *Fortunella margarita* (金橘) or round *F. japonica* (圓金橘). They are grown as pot plants, specifically for the Chinese New Year when the fruits signify "gold", and therefore, wealth. A well-proportioned plant is a delight to behold, packed with its golden fruits. It is a very important commercial plant at this time, sold everywhere and seen everywhere—in homes, hotel lobbies, shops and public places. Although primarily raised for ornament, the fruit is edible. It is almost never eaten fresh but makes a tasty traditional sweet preserve. It is also used for medicinal purposes and is said to be very soothing for the throat. A decent marmalade can also be made from it.

The abundance of these shrubs in Chinese New Year markets would suggest that kumquat is an easy plant to grow. This has not been my experience, however. Kumquat culture is the result of very expert cultivation and long tradition. There is no harm in trying your hand, though. Start off by purchasing a mature fruiting plant. When its ornamental use is over, prune moderately to remove the fruits and to produce new, bushier growth. The first crop of fragrant white flowers should be removed. When a second crop appears, feed regularly with peanut cake until the fruits are well established. The plants also require re-potting each year, pruning the roots, shaking off the old soil and replacing with rich, fresh loam. Propagation is by grafting, usually onto a lemon rootstock.

Lantana 馬纓丹屬

Lantana sp.

This genus of the verbena family consists of 150 species of shrubs and perennials, many of which are notorious weeds.

The wild **common lantana** (馬纓丹屬／臭草, *Lantana camara*) is a ubiquitous, irregular, thorny shrub generally regarded as a troublesome weed in Hong Kong. If it finds nearby support, it will readily scramble up 4–5 m with its woody, thorny canes and even invade neighbouring trees. The leaves are rough to the touch, ovate, 3 cm long with a toothed margin and give off a pungent odour when crushed. Weed it may be, but I find the flowers very attractive. The tiny multicoloured flowers in red, orange, pink and yellow come together to form small domed heads about 3 cm across. The flowers go on to produce fruit in the form of green berries, later ripening to black. As young boys, my friends and I found the unripe berries very useful as ammunition for pea-shooters. We did not know then that the berries contained a poison that would result in a huge bellyache if swallowed! There are numerous cultivars which are usually unarmed, some with the multicoloured heads as mentioned above, and some in single colours—purple, yellow or white. Flowers are produced all year long but cultivars do not fruit as readily as the wild version. These are now commonly seen in parks and private gardens as very attractive shrubs that show no inclination to becoming weedy. Propagation is by seed sown in autumn or by cuttings in spring or summer.

The **trailing lantana** (蔓馬纓丹, *L. montevidensis* syn. *L. selloviana*) is a small evergreen shrub which has become very widespread in Hong Kong gardens. All year round, but especially in spring and early summer, it produces flowery heads of tiny purple flowers similar to *L. camara*. This lantana has a trailing habit and is most useful as ground cover or to plant at the base of a tree. It also makes a colourful pot plant and its sprawl makes it attractive in hanging baskets or when planted to spill over banks and walls. Lantana should be grown in a sunny position but it is not particular about soil. A hard pruning in January is beneficial. Old plants may look scraggly with dense, tangled branches. These should be discarded and replaced by new plants raised in similar fashion to *L. camara*.

Trailing lantana

Larkspur (delphinium) 飛燕草
Delphinium

Larkspur (*Delphinium consolida*) is the annual variety and "delphinium", as a common name, usually refers to the various perennial species. Both may be grown in Hong Kong, the delphinium being treated as an annual. These tall, stately plants are excellent as a backdrop for other plants. A succession of flowers in blue, pink or white is borne in profusion on spikes up to 1 m high. The leaves are finely cut, fern-like, with a soft, feathery appearance. They are good cut flowers. A dwarf species growing to about 50 cm high is also available. These flowers are not easy to raise. They dislike transplanting and should be sown where they are to grow. Germination is slow and sometimes erratic. The tall spikes fall easy victim to strong winds and so should only be grown in a sheltered site with adequate sun. Light staking may be required. Autumn-sown plants flower in the spring usually at Easter time.

Leek 大蒜
Allium porrum

Leek is an onion relative that does not form a distinct bulb and has a mild flavour. The white stem-like portion is made up of concentric layers of the leaf bases. Leek should be sown in October or November. However, a sowing in spring is also possible. I have seen farms harvesting good-quality leeks as late in the season as June. The seeds should be sown in pans and when the seedlings are large enough to handle, transfer to 7-cm plastic pots. Grow on until 10 cm high before planting in their permanent growing positions with the plants 15 cm apart. Leeks like a good-draining rich soil with a heavy organic content. When close to maturing, heap earth up around the bases to blanch them. Leeks have a relatively long growing period, so choose an early maturing variety if possible.

Lettuce (and Cichorium) 生菜
Lactuca sativa

This widespread genus of about 100 species includes a number of common weeds, but is best known in the form of the common lettuce, *Lactuca sativa*. It is an ancient vegetable, probably derived from the weedy "prickly lettuce" *L. serriola*, and is known to have been in cultivation for 5000 years. It comes in two main types, the **heading** or **cabbage variety** with a well formed heart, or the **loose leaf variety**. If left to flower, it will be evident that lettuce is of the daisy family, with large sprays of small, daisy-like blooms, white, yellow or mauve.

Cos lettuce "Little Gem"

Leaf lettuce, rather than the heading variety, is more suited to Hong Kong. The heading varieties such as "Iceberg", prefer much cooler conditions, and although they can be grown, the heads have some difficulty in reaching a good size. The common wet market "local" leaf lettuce is actually grown mostly from Italian seed. Almost any type of leaf lettuce will succeed, although I have found the red variety such as "Red Oak" to be rather fussy and slow to take off. Cos or Romaine lettuce does very well. I can recommend my particular favourite, the dwarf Cos "Little Gem". This beautiful, crisp lettuce grows only to about 15 cm tall and I grow these every year in 10-cm pots, one to a pot. These attractive little pot plants make nice gifts.

The large number of cultivars available means that lettuce comes in many leaf forms, with different textures and tastes. I try to look for something new to grow each year. Another idea is to mix seeds of different varieties and sow them together, resulting in a mixed bag at harvest time.

Sow the seeds thinly, from September through to March. If sown in pans, transplant into small plastic pots, one to each pot, when the second leaf has appeared. Alternatively start directly in these 7-cm plastic pots, four seeds to a pot, then thinning to retain one healthy seedling. Allow to grow to 7 cm high before setting out in beds. Keep the plants 25 cm apart each way.

Lettuce is great in containers, succeeding in 21- or even 15-cm pots. Lettuce is also a good filler, utilising any odd bits of space in the garden or planted in between other later maturing plants such as cabbage. The local variety is ready for picking in about 10 weeks, but the heading lettuce will take about 15 weeks. Lettuce can be grown in any moist soil with good drainage, in full sun or part shade. It is a cool season vegetable, and notwithstanding the claims of certain "all season" lettuce, it is best to avoid cultivation in the hot summers. There are two exceptions mentioned below that will do well in the summer.

Note should be taken of some unusual lettuce varieties sold in local wet markets. One such variety is **stem lettuce** or **celtuce** (窩菜, *L. sativa* var. Augustana). The plant has a swollen stem which is the part to be eaten. It is crunchy in texture with a mild celery taste, and can be eaten raw or stir-fried.

This is a good time to bring up the subject of *Cichorium*, since it is often confused with lettuce or *Lactuca*—which is not surprising since the two are in fact closely related. This conundrum will become clearer as you continue reading.

An interesting vegetable known locally as "**fu muk choi**" 苦墨菜, has long, broad, tongue-shaped leaves. It is occasionally seen in wet markets where it is regarded as a rather coarse vegetable with a bitter hint. A slightly more delicate variety with angled or cut leaves, "**yau muk choi**" 油墨菜 is very similar but less bitter to the palate. Both of these plants grow on erect main stems with basal tufts of leaves appearing continually so that one sowing will last the whole season. The leaves are plucked for use as required. The flowers are white, dandelion-like, and self-seeding is common. These two varieties can be grown throughout the year, even in the summer. They are, therefore, extremely useful for summer salads when the usual lettuce is not available in the garden. Eat the leaves raw, thinly shredded with an olive oil dressing, or cook them the Cantonese way—stir-fry.

Fu muk choi:
Lactuca chinensis

Determining the proper nomenclature for fu muk choi had been something of an obsession for me, largely because nobody seemed to be able to shed any light on the subject. I consulted many knowledgeable local sources, only to be disappointed in receiving different answers each time.

For some years now, from time to time (although I cannot remember just how it all started), I have been supplying fu muk choi to a community of Italian sisters who are always delighted to receive what they called their favourite "cicoria", that is, *Cichorium. C. intybus* is grown extensively in France, Belgium, and especially Italy, where it has a firm place in the cuisine of these countries. It takes the form of small lettuces varying greatly in leaf form and colour including many that have strong purple or red tones. With this Italian input, it was quite natural for me, therefore, to regard fu muk choi as one of the many varieties of *C.*

intybus. Some doubts remained, however, because fu muk choi is also listed in several reference works as *Sonchus oleracea* and *Youngia denticulata*. However, these are described as weedy plants, gathered in the wild for use as potherbs, whereas fu muk choi is a vegetable cultivated in southern China, and shows no weedy features. On the other hand, some books and seed vendors regard fu muk choi as a form of lettuce or *Lactuca*.

There was eventually a happy conclusion to my dilemma when I was privileged to meet the world-renowned botanist, Professor Shiu-ying Hu, author of *Food Plants of China* (2005). Confronted with a potted specimen of fu muk choi, Professor Hu instantly made a positive identification: *Lactuca chinensis*, thus bringing my years-long odyssey to an end.

The other species of *Cichorium* is *C. endivia*, the popular salad vegetable endive, with finely-divided, crisp, bitter leaves. Chicory, with its hearted heads (known as chicons) also belongs in this group.

Cichorium intybus "Zuccherina di Trieste"

Lily turf

Lily turf 山麥冬
Liriope spicata

Those familiar with our countryside will readily recognise this wild flower which is found in damp wooded areas, often in deep shade. Tufts of long, narrow, stiff, dark green leaves grow from a rhizome or underground stem. In summer, flowering spikes appear, carrying small lavender-coloured flowers (and vaguely resembling the flowers of lavender). Its fruit are small berries, produced in great numbers, green at first, later turning black.

Lily turf is perhaps not as popular in gardens as it deserves to be. Its preference for shade is its greatest usefulness, as it will grow where no other flowering plants will survive. Grow lily turf in rock gardens, shady corners or around the base of trees. Even when out of flower the plant remains attractive for its foliage. It needs little care. Propagation is easiest by division of the rhizome, although it can also be raised from seed.

The rhizomes are used in traditional medicine as an anti-tussive, expectorant and emollient.

Lobelia 半邊蓮
Lobelia sp.

A large group of annuals, perennials and shrubs mainly used for bedding, edging, rock gardens or hanging baskets. The best variety for Hong Kong is a compact annual about 20 cm in height, bearing flowers of varying colours in fair profusion. Each flower is basically tubular, expanding out to a three- to five-lobed lip. Sow the seeds in pans from September to November. When 5 cm high, transplant clumps of four or five seedlings to a sunny flowering site.

Loquat 枇杷
Eriobotrya japonica

You may not want to grow the Chinese loquat (or Japanese plum) for its fruit, but did you know that it makes a handsome pot plant? Take the pit from a fresh loquat, soak it in water for 24 hours, then plant in a 25-cm pot with good soil and free drainage. It germinates without fuss. Water plentifully and feed once a month. The plant has large, pointed, grey-green leaves that look embossed because the leaf surface bulges slightly between the veins. Tolerant of shade, it is useful as an indoor ornamental.

Maranta (rabbit tracks, prayer plant) 花葉竹芋

Maranta leuconeura

A small perennial evergreen with leafy stems, grown for its ornamental foliage. The cultivar "Kerchoviana" has brown markings on the leaves resembling rabbits' footprints, and is sometimes referred to by the common name of "rabbit tracks". "Erythroneura" has a herringbone pattern of pink veins on velvety dark green leaves. Its habit of standing its leaves upright at night gives it another name, "prayer plant". Grow Maranta indoors in bright open shade. It grows quite rapidly and needs regular trimming. Feed fortnightly with a liquid fertiliser such as fish emulsion. Pot on as required or else divide for propagation.

Marigold 萬壽菊

Tagetes sp.

This ever-popular, colourful annual is arguably the easiest of the flowering annuals to grow. It is probably the most reliable way for a quick colour fix in the garden, matched only, perhaps, by busy lizzie.

The tall **African marigold** (*Tagetes lucida*) grows to about 60 cm with dome-shaped flowers usually yellow or orange. The dwarf **French marigold** (*T. patula*) reaches 30 cm and comes in a range of colours from bright yellow to a dark rust with many shades and mixtures in between.

Marigolds are best sown from September to November. However, they are very adaptable and can be sown much earlier, say in July, to colour the garden in the autumn months when not many other flowering annuals are in season. Marigolds are versatile, attractive *en masse* in beds or in pots. Sow the seeds in pans 1 cm deep. The seedlings appear in four or five days and are usually quite sturdy. When the second leaf appears, transplant individually into small 7-cm pots. Make the final transplantation to the flowering site when 7 cm tall. If the first buds appear when the plants are still small, pinch them out to encourage bushy growth. Dead-head regularly to prolong the flowering period.

French marigold

Marigolds are a natural deterrent to insects and nematodes, and may be planted in various parts of the vegetable garden (inter-planting) for this purpose. Note, however, that marigolds themselves are popular with snails and slugs. These pests should be dealt with accordingly. (See "Pests".)

Marvel of Peru (four o'clock plant) 紫茉莉

Mirabilis jalapa

This perennial, grown as an annual, has erect stems and heart-shaped, mid-green leaves. Its flowers are in various colours—magenta, red, yellow, pink and white and are slightly fragrant. The flowers are trumpet-shaped with a long stem. Its name "four o'clock plant" comes from the fact that it opens in the afternoon to close and fade at dawn. The flowers last only a day but are produced in rapid succession. An interesting plant though not particularly visually arresting. It is grown from seed sown in spring and flowers from April to October.

Matrimony vine (Chinese boxthorn, Chinese wolfberry) 枸杞

Lycium chinense

I have never been able to discover how this native of China received its intriguing name. Apparently the name did not originate in China. It was more likely coined by Europeans several centuries ago. However, matrimony vine has never established itself in the European or North American cuisines. An alternative name is the Chinese boxthorn, although it is now more fashionable to refer to it as wolfberry. It is a thorny shrub about 1 m tall with dark green ovate leaves. The fruit is an oval, bright orange-red berry about 1.5 cm long. The dried berries are sold in Chinese groceries for use in many types of herbal soup. It has long been used in traditional Chinese medicine for its health giving properties. In recent years, western health food enthusiasts have embraced the wolfberry as a sort of panacea, extolling its alleged roles as an immune system stimulant, an antioxidant, and as an aid to longevity. It is now promoted in numerous forms: juice, tablets, powders and so on. The fresh stalks are easily bought at wet markets for use as a vegetable, but only the leaves are eaten. Grow this plant from cuttings in autumn from any fresh stem bought from the market. Alternatively, raise from seed in September.

The leaves make a healthy light soup. The leaves need to be stripped from the stems and it is necessary to be very careful while doing this since the thorns can inflict a painful wound.

Matrimony vine soup 枸杞湯

<u>Ingredients</u>
- 2 handfuls matrimony vine leaves
- 150 g fresh pork liver, sliced (or 250 mL chicken stock)
- 1/2 handful dried matrimony vine berries (wolfberries), soaked for 15 mins.
- Knob of ginger
- 1 egg
- 1.5 L water

<u>Method</u>
- Very lightly sauté the liver with a knob of ginger in a little vegetable oil.
- Add the water and bring to a boil.
- Toss in the matrimony vine leaves and the wolfberries. Bring back to the boil for 2 mins.
- Stir in a beaten egg and your soup is done.
- For those who have no stomach for liver, substitute 250 mL of chicken stock.
- By the way, capsicum leaves may be substituted for matrimony vine leaves with a very similar result.

Mock lime 米仔蘭

Aglaia odorata

This much-branched southeast Asian evergreen shrub has shiny, dense, dark-green foliage and clusters of tiny flowers appearing in summer. It is very popular in private gardens and parks because of the fragrance of its flowers and because it does well in containers. It tolerates frequent pruning and can be used as a hedge. Its dense foliage also makes it useful as a screen. Sprays of foliage may be used in flower arrangements, and the flowers can be used to flavour tea. In traditional medicine mock lime has been used as an antidepressive. Propagate by cuttings in spring and summer.

Monstera 蓬萊蕉

Monstera deliciosa

A favourite evergreen climber grown for its massive, dark green leaves which are curiously cut and variously perforated. Pot-grown plants should be made to climb around a central stake covered with bark or coconut matting. Prominent trailing aerial roots that develop should be directed back into the soil. Outdoor specimens grow best in filtered sunlight or open shade, and may grow into massive, striking plants, climbing up tree trunks or rough walls. Aerial roots that reach the soil develop into sturdy supports for large plants. The flowers are densely packed into a spike which is surrounded by a large white bract or spathe. The fruit is said to be delicious (hence its name) but I have never dared try it myself.

M

Mock lime

Morning glory (See also "Water spinach") 五爪金龍

Ipomea sp.

This is a large group of annual and perennial vines flowering in the summer. All share the same common name. In Hong Kong, the most familiar of the wild perennials is *Ipomea cairica* (五爪金龍) which has bright purple flowers with a deeper-coloured throat. The corolla is funnel-shaped with five completely fused petals. Its rapacious and aggressive growth habit is aptly reflected in its Chinese name—"five-clawed golden dragon". Generally regarded as a weed, morning glory is often seen indiscriminately enveloping everything within its reach. Among the other wild species are *I. leari* (藍牽牛花, blue dawn flower) with delicate blue flowers and *I. brasiliensis* (海灘牽牛). The latter also goes by the name of beach morning glory, since it is a coastal plant usually seen scrambling over beaches and shorelines.

Blue dawn flower

The garden varieties are grown from seed and come in a wider spectrum of colours than their wild cousins. The seeds are faceted and very hard. They may be nicked with a knife or soaked in hot water for two hours before planting to hasten germination. Set the young plants out in a sunny position, 20 cm apart. Best used for trellises, fences, ground cover or to cascade over a bank. No feeding is necessary.

Mussaenda 白紙扇

Mussaenda philippica

A good-looking, medium-sized shrub native to tropical and subtropical regions, producing in summer large masses of pink or white blooms. The flowers are insignificant and small. The colour is provided by a large pink sepal enlarged to a sort of bract. A white variety is also available. In January or February, prune severely to 15 cm from the ground. Propagate by air layering. A wild white variety (野白紙扇, *Mussaenda erosa*) is sometimes seen in our

Nasturtium 旱金蓮

Tropaeolum majus

This is a tough, dependable annual of a trailing or climbing habit with bright orange or yellow flowers. It is favoured as a pot plant or for planting in beds. Because of its quick growth and sprawling habit, it may be used as ground cover, especially for vacant lots or hillsides where the soil is lean. Poor soil brings out the best in nasturtium: an over-rich soil encourages foliage at the expense of flowers. Nasturtium loves the sun and will not compromise with shade. The leaves are fresh-looking, mid-green, circular, slightly cupped with radial veins. The surface of the leaves is coated with a wax which makes them well-nigh unwettable. After a rainstorm (or watering), liquid globules of water collect in the leaves making a very pretty sight. The flowers are trumpet-shaped, five-petalled, spurred and faintly scented. There are several varieties with single or double flowers and a compact or trailing habit. They last well as cut flowers. Both the leaves and flowers give off a characteristic pungent odour when crushed. The seeds, flowers and leaves can be used as food flavouring and eaten in salads. It is hot and peppery in taste, very similar to watercress (西洋菜, *Nasturtium officinale*) to which it is closely related.

The seed is quite large and should be sown directly into the pot or bed in which it is to flower. Sowing is best done in October. Nasturtium grown as ground cover will self-seed and reappear on its own the following year. Pot grown plants may need some form of light support, for example, a loose dome made of bent bamboo strips.

Never-never plant 錦竹芋

Ctenanthe oppenheimiana

Pronounce *Ctenanthe* with the "C" silent. These plants, from Brazil, are sometimes confused with Maranta or *Calathea* to which they are related. They grow to about 60 cm tall and are valued for their interesting foliage. The long leaves, about 25 cm, are slightly oblong with a herring-bone pattern of blotchy cream and green with red undersides. They grow in open shade or part sun and are popular as borders. A faster growing *C. lubbersiana* is green and cream without the red highlights. Propagation is best by using basal offshoots.

Nicotiana (tobacco flower) 煙草花

Nicotiana sp.

The 60-odd species in this genus includes the commercial tobacco plant. I do love this tall erect perennial, grown as an annual in Hong Kong. *Nicotiana* x *sanderae* or *N. alata* are equally beautiful. You have a choice of dwarf or tall varieties. All produce masses and masses of flowers, in loose clusters, red-carmine, cream, white, purple and yellow. The flowers are tubular, flaring out, trumpet-like into five pointed lobes. *Nicotiana* is suitable for beds, planters or pots. Most varieties are scented at night unless grown in the shade. They may be used as cut flowers, but the stems and leaves are slightly sticky to handle. Sow the seeds in October. Grow in rich, well-drained soil, in full or partial sun. Staking may be necessary for the taller varieties. Dead-heading prolongs the production of flowers.

Night-blooming jasmine (lady of the night) 夜丁香

Cestrum nocturnum

The night-blooming jasmine gives off a scent so heady that many people cannot tolerate it. I find it agreeable in small doses. A large bush can be overwhelming, which is why I only keep a single pot-grown specimen, frequently pruned to limit its size. Even then its perfume can be detected from a long way off. Night-blooming jasmine is a medium-sized shrub producing, in summer, small tubular white flowers that are not very eye-catching. The scraggly shrub is not particularly handsome either, but this is not important since it is really grown for its fragrance. At night the flowers open to release their intense perfume, which I liken to the once-popular Yardley's brilliantine used for grooming hair. No scent is given out during the day. It is not very particular about its growth requirements and needs little care. It grows well in pots, which then can be moved out of the way when the flowering period is over. Prune after each flowering, and pinch out the growing tips to create a bushy effect. New plants can be easily raised from cuttings taken at almost any time of the year.

Norfolk Island pine 南洋杉

Araucaria heterophylla

This South Pacific native belongs to a genus of geologically ancient conifers. It is a stately, magnificent evergreen, at its best when allowed to grow to its full height of 60–70 m. In the days of sail, the straight trunks were sought after as masts for ships. It succeeds admirably in Hong Kong and is now becoming more popular in private gardens. It has not figured much in the very active tree-planting programmes we have seen in Hong Kong in recent years, and I don't know why. Despite its great height, I have never seen one fall in a typhoon. Young trees, grown in containers even as small as 25-cm pots, make effective pot plants, growing up to 2 m. It can be raised from seed but young trees are also readily available at garden shops.

Okra (lady's fingers, gumbo) 羊角豆／毛茄
Hibiscus esculentus

Exculentus means succulent, delicious. Therefore, any genus name followed by *esculentus* means some part of that plant is good to eat. Okra is thus delicious *Hibiscus*. And just by looking at their scientific names, you will know that *Manihot esculenta* (tapioca) and *Lycopersicon esculentum* (tomato) are food plants.

Not many people know about this vegetable, and fewer still use it in the kitchen. It is thought to have originated in Africa and was apparently brought to the Americas in the slave trade about three centuries ago. It is indeed a fine summer crop. The okra pods are, in a word, delicious. A heat-loving plant, it thrives in our blistering summers. Okra is a tall, stately plant up to 2 m. Being a *Hibiscus*, it has beautiful flowers, a light yellow colour. These are attractive plants in their own right and would not be out of place as a backdrop to ornamentals. The deeply dissected leaves bear a vague resemblance to cannabis, and not a few passers-by have enquired about the legality of my crop! The flowers give way to pods, each resembling an erect chilli. The growth rate of these pods is truly amazing. A pod too young to be picked in the morning may be ready in the afternoon. Pick them when young, about 7–8 cm long when they are at their best. The pods are covered with fine stiff hairs which can occasionally irritate the skin—so be gentle with the picking, or wear gloves. Old pods are very fibrous and cannot be eaten.

I have grown okra every summer for the last twenty years. "Long Green" or "Clemson Spineless" are equally good varieties, though "Spineless" has the advantage of being without the prickly hairs. Four or five plants are all you need to keep you in good supply. If you have more than you can eat, then consider freezing some. They keep well for about three months.

Start okra in April through July. Resist any attempt to sow earlier, as warmth is essential to the young seedlings. The seeds may be sown directly in the growing site, three seeds to a drill 2 cm deep. When the seedlings are established, keep the strongest plant and thin out the other two. The mature plants should have at least half a metre between them. The seeds may

also be sown in a 10-cm pot, four seeds to each pot. This is my own preferred method. April and May can bring heavy rains and pot-grown seedlings can be conveniently taken to shelter. Transplant out when 15 cm high. Very little setback in growth results from this technique. Grow in full sun and water copiously. Verandah-grown plants need a pot not smaller than 30 cm in size, and should have no less than three hours of sunshine a day. Leave a few pods to go to seed for propagation the following year. These pods should be left on the plant until they become thoroughly hardened and brown. Each pod may contain a hundred seeds.

Before cooking, the hairs should be scraped off with the edge of a knife. Both the pods and the seeds have a mucilaginous consistency, useful for thickening stews or soups. It is tasty as a quick stir-fry in butter or olive oil. Undoubtedly the best use of okra is in a curry. What follows is a really simple curry that can be whipped up in a jiffy.

Okra and minced beef (or lamb) curry 毛茄咖喱

<u>Ingredients</u>

- 15 okras (whole)
- 250 g minced beef or lamb
- 3 cloves garlic
- 2 medium onions
- 3 dried red chillies
- 1 can chopped tomatoes
- 1 knob ginger, chopped
- 1 tbs. each of garam marsala, coriander powder and cumin powder
- 1 sprig curry leaves (if available—have you grown your own?)
- 1 tbs. butter

<u>Method</u>

- Fry the ginger, garlic, chillies and onions until the onions are soft but not coloured.
- Mix in a can of chopped tomatoes.
- Transfer the mixture to a blender and blend thoroughly.
- Return the mixture to the pan, add the garam marsala, coriander powder, cumin powder, butter, curry leaves and the minced meat. Salt to taste.
- Cook for 15 mins., add the okras and cook for another 15 mins.
- A small tub of yoghurt added at this stage is optional.

Oleander 夾竹桃

Nerium indicum

A beautiful evergreen shrub, native to tropical and subtropical Asia, growing to 3–4 m tall. It is frequently seen in public gardens and roadsides. Oleander is usually many-stemmed, but can be trained into a single-stemmed tree. Its leaves are narrow, dark green and leathery. Flowers are produced year-round, though mostly in summer, and may be pink or white, single or double, with a distinctive, subtle fragrance. The shrub is very attractive in all seasons and is highly recommended to anyone with sufficient space for it. It may also be tried in large containers. There are no particular soil or drainage requirements as long as there is full sun. It should be noted that the sap is poisonous. Prunings and fallen leaves should be properly disposed of and should not be used in barbeque fires. Propagation by cuttings.

Oleander, yellow 黃花夾竹桃
Thevetia peruviana

A small tree, indigenous to South America, commonly cultivated in Hong Kong. The evergreen, shiny green leaves are narrow, lanceolate, 7–10 cm long. From a distance, the foliage has a delicate, feathery appearance. The rich-yellow flowers appear throughout the summer, scattered singly and evenly throughout the tree. They later give rise to odd-shaped fleshy green fruit with prominent ridges. Like its oleander relative, *Nerium*, its sap is poisonous.

Orange jessamine (mock orange) 九里香
Murraya paniculata

This medium-sized shrub is easily mistaken at a distance for mock lime (*Aglaia odorata*). Closer examination, however, shows the plant is made up of shinier, darker green leaflets, arranged densely. Clusters of small creamy white flowers appear at the branch tips from April to August. Its Chinese name "fragrant from a distance of nine miles" is an indication of the intensity of its scent. It is allied to *Citrus* which explains its common names of mock orange or orange jessamine. Propagate from cuttings in spring and summer.

Orchids 蘭科

The widespread belief that orchids are difficult to grow and require constant care is fortunately not true. In fact, orchids can be grown quite easily in the ordinary home environment provided certain conditions of light, humidity and temperature are met. Suitably cared for, plants can bloom for many years.

Orchids form probably the largest flowering plant family. About half the species grow on the ground and are known as **terrestrial** orchids while the other half cling on trees and rocks and are known as **epiphytic**. Most cultivated house plant varieties are epiphytic. In addition to a conventional root system at the base, epiphytic orchids usually have aerial roots whose function is to enable the plant to creep and cling to support.

The growth of epiphytic orchids follows one of two patterns. **Monopodial** or one-footed orchids (e.g. *Vanda*) give out a single main stem from a tuft of roots at the base. Leaves clothe the length of the stem and flower stalks are given out between leaf axils near the top. The second pattern of growth is **sympodial**, in which many stems arise from a horizontally growing rhizome. The thick stems, called pseudobulbs, act as storage organs to maintain the plants through periods of drought.

Orchid leaves vary greatly in shape, size and thickness. No generalisations can be made. Orchid flowers, on the other hand, all follow a fixed pattern of six symmetrically arranged petal-like segments. The uppermost segment and the lower two twin segments are alike in shape, colour and size, and are known as sepals. The two twin segments flanking the uppermost sepals are larger than the others which they otherwise resemble closely. These are called

O

petals. The remaining sixth segment is always radically different and is called the lip. A central reproductive column completes the flower. Having said that the flowers have a fixed pattern, one can now marvel at how this fixed pattern can result in the vast variations of shapes, sizes and colours that make the orchid family so fascinating.

Pot-grown orchids must be free-draining. For terrestrial orchids, a mixture of gravel or perlite, coarse peat and loam is suitable. Conventional clay pots may be used. Epiphytic orchids can be grown on slabs of osmunda fibre. For convenience, prepared potting mixes can also be bought. Epiphytic orchids prefer special perforated clay pots, slatted wood or wire baskets.

Orchids should be grown in filtered light. A few hours of direct sunlight, especially in the cold season, is helpful. High humidity is also a requirement. Spray hanging plants frequently, or stand pots in trays of moistened peat. Watering, however, must never be excessive, this being the commonest cause of failure. The plant should be fairly dry before watering, even if this means an interval of a week.

Sympodial orchids are propagated by division of the rhizome, each section containing two or three pseudobulbs. Monopodial orchids can be propagated by side shoot or tip cuttings containing a few aerial roots.

I am not a great orchid gardener and I keep only the sure-fire, easy-care varieties such as *Cymbidium* (四季蘭), dancing lady orchid (跳舞蘭, *Oncidium*), and nun's orchid (鶴頂蘭, *Phaius tankerville*). I find greater delight in chance encounters with wild orchids on my frequent walks in the hills; among these, the buttercup orchid (苞唇蘭 / 牛油杯, *Spathoglottis pubescens*) and the bamboo orchid (竹蘭, *Arundina chinensis*).

Nun's orchid

Osmanthus 桂花

Osmanthus fragrans

This is a medium-sized cultivated shrub, rather irregular in its branching habit. It is not an elegant plant, with rough, leathery leaves, and characteristically greyish stems. Its insignificant white flowers are very small and appear in clusters at the leaf axils. But what a delightful fragrance. This, after all, is what it is grown for. Propagate by cuttings.

In traditional medicine, osmanthus is used as an expectorant, antitussive and antirheumatic.

Oyster plant 蚌花

Rhoeo discolor

This is a low herbaceous shrub from South America with a height and spread of about 25 cm. It is grown for its colourful green leaves tinged with red below. The leaves are thick, sword-shaped. The small white flowers are enclosed in two bracts resembling an oyster. Suitable for borders, rock gardens and shady areas. Propagate by taking cuttings of basal shoots and inserting into small pots of potting soil.

Pak choi (Chinese white cabbage) 白菜
Brassica chinensis

Flowering hearts of pak choi

This could be the easiest to grow of the local Chinese vegetables. It is also one of the tastiest and one of the most popular. More than any other Chinese vegetable, it has made its mark in the western world where it is often known as "bok choy". Sow the seeds in pans from July to January. Transplant to beds when 7 cm high, spacing the plants 10–15 cm apart each way depending on which variety is being grown. Feed with a dilute liquid fertiliser every two weeks. The plants are quick growing and may be harvested in about eight weeks. To prolong the period of supply, do not harvest the plants whole, but pick and use the outer leaves as required, leaving the plants to bolt eventually. The bolting, flower-bearing heart (白菜心) is the tastiest part of the vegetable. Another strategy is to sow thinly, broadcast, and to thin out as the plants begin to crowd. The thinnings can be used for the table. If you have a large crop, try drying some of it for later use. Note, though, that only the tall "little pak choi" (see below) is suitable for drying. Dried pak choi (白菜乾) is a popular item in the markets, usually used for making a delicious and refreshing soup. Pull the plants whole and cut away the roots. Blanch them in boiling water, then dry in the sun in a basket or strung along a clothes line. In good weather, two days will be sufficient. The dried vegetable can be kept for months. When needed in the kitchen, soak in hot water for an hour before using.

Pak choi

There are two common varieties of pak choi. Paradoxically, the so-called "**little**" **pak choi** (小白菜) is the tall version, growing to about 20 cm, while the "**big**" **pak choi** (大白菜) is the dwarf version with broader, more succulent leaf petioles, and growing to about 10 cm. Still another variety, now hugely popular, is the green or **Shanghai pak choi** (上海白菜). Here, the leaf petioles are green and less fleshy, being rather thinner and slightly spoon-shaped. In restaurants, Shanghai pak choi sometimes has its leaves cut away, leaving only the clustered leaf blades to be served at table.

Palms 葵

There is something about palms that is at once graceful and soothing, evoking a warm, tropical ambience. The large outdoor palms, now planted in very large numbers in public places, are either the **Alexandra** or **king palm** (假檳榔, *Archonotrophoenix alexandrae*) or the **royal palm** (王棕, *Roystonea regia*). Both are tall and stately but can be easily distinguished. The Alexandra palm has graceful trunks with a regular gentle taper, whereas the Royal palm usually has a curious bulge somewhere in the middle. These are large plants and best suited for public gardens. Nevertheless, an Alexandra palm appeared out of nowhere in my garden one day and is now growing beautifully in a deep planter which, unfortunately, it will eventually outgrow.

The quintessential potted palm is the **bamboo palm** (散尾葵, *Chrysalidocarpus lutescens*), seen everywhere from homes to hotel lobbies. It is tolerant of shade and appreciates protection from harsh winds—hence ideally suited to indoors. As it grows in size, it should be potted on in spring, but even with confined roots it grows well. A large dragon urn will support a large luxuriant specimen 3 m high, very suitable for entrances, doorways, etc. It is not particular as to soil but drainage must be good. Grown outdoors, it forms clumps with several trunks arising from the base and can reach considerable height, about 5–6 m. The feathery fronds are mid- to dark-green, almost always with a slight yellow tinge around the tips. It is prone to scale infestation. As the fronds detach, they leave ring marks on an otherwise smooth stem, giving it a resemblance to bamboo.

Lady palm (棕竹, *Rhapis*) is a genus of slow-growing palms originating in Thailand and southern China. They grow in clumps and produce fan-shaped foliage, reaching a height of a metre or more. The deep green leaves are deeply divided lengthwise into almost entirely separate segments, resulting in a frond-like appearance. The trunks are covered with a net of brown fibrous sheaths. Excellent for containers and shady areas.

Lady palm

Fishtail palm (魚尾葵, *Caryota ochlandra*) is becoming very popular in public places because of its ease of cultivation and rapid growth. Small specimens may be raised in containers but need to be potted on frequently to keep pace with its growth. Outdoors, it is a plant of considerable character. Large feathery fronds are produced from a single main trunk. Each leaf broadens out, ending obliquely and slightly split to resemble a fishtail. The flowers are large inflorescences appearing in spring and producing a huge amount of seeds. Self-seeded plants appear in large numbers and can be dug up to be planted on.

Fishtail palm

Chinese fan palm (蒲葵, *Livistonia chinensis*) can develop to a fair-sized tree if grown outdoors. Pot-grown, it remains as a shrub, almost stemless with the leaves sprouting from a fibrous core. The leaves are large, fan-shaped with their edges deeply cut to produce a drooping fringe. Traditional Chinese fans are made from these leaves.

The **dwarf date palm** (軟葉刺葵, *Phoenix roebelenii*) is a small tree very popular in parks and public gardens. A small specimen can be maintained in a large container for many years.

The **sago palm** (鳳尾松, *Cycas revoluta*) has a short stout trunk, sometimes multiple, growing 1–2 m high. The fronds are quite characteristic, forming a dense crown of stiff, pinnate leaves with a sharp spiky tip. It is highly ornamental, often used as a feature in an open space. Also successful as a container plant.

The **parlour palm** (袖珍椰子, *Chamaedorea elegans*) is a slow-growing palm resembling a miniature bamboo palm. It is grown mainly as an indoor pot plant because of its manageable size and because it does well in shade.

Pansy 三色堇

Viola tricolor

An old-fashioned garden favourite, admired for its dwarf habit and lovely flowers. Popular for edgings, rock gardens, pots, and also as cut flowers. The velvety blooms of pansy come in many vivid colours, very often several colours in brilliant contrast. The flowers have five petals in a flat-faced arrangement. The slow-growing plant is compact, reaching only about 15 cm in height. The leaves are oval with a blunt-toothed edge. Sow the small seeds from September to November in pans. Exclusion of light for about seven days hastens germination. Transplant the seedlings into small plastic pots and then out to the flowering site which may be in full sun or part shade. Remove withered blooms regularly. Try using the colourful petals as an unusual garnish in a green salad.

Papaya 木瓜
Carica papaya

This is a true favourite of mine, a small tree that grows easily and bears tasty, versatile fruit. Originally from Central and South America, it is now grown throughout the tropics. The trunk is single, with characteristic markings from scars left by the fallen leaves. These leaves should always be allowed to drop off naturally and should not be trimmed away as this affects fruit production. The leaves are large and deeply dissected. A white sticky latex exudes from any damaged part of the plant. There are separate male and female trees, worthwhile fruits coming only from the female. The female flowers appear singly at the leaf axils and almost every one is followed by a fruit. The male tree produces abundant flowers and small elongated fruits of poor quality. For this reason, male trees are discarded as soon as they are recognised, unless of course you are a gourmet with an acquired taste for the male flowers. The flowers are extremely bitter, but if properly prepared, it has an interesting flavour which few people have sampled. The flowers should be blanched in boiling water, discarding the water at least twice, thus removing the bitter taste. They are delicious stir-fried with meat or with a shrimp paste. When unripe, the fruit is a tasty vegetable. The partly ripe fruit makes an excellent soup, naturally sweetened by the ripening portions. The fully ripe fruit is the familiar tropical delicacy everybody loves. The home gardener has the distinct advantage of having tree-ripened fruit which is vastly superior to the forced-ripened market specimens.

Papaya: male flowers

Papaya contains papain and chymopapain, two enzymes that are used as meat tenderiser. Adding a generous slice of ripe or partly ripe papaya to cook with a stew significantly softens the meat. You must try it to believe it. These enzymes are also used in the pharmaceutical industry as an effective treatment for inflammation and swelling.

In spring, sow the fresh seed taken from a good quality, tree-ripened papaya. Germination is rapid and dependable. Transfer three strong seedlings to harden in a 25-cm pot. When well established, retain the strongest plant and discard the others. Grow in a sunny site but remove to safety in heavy rains or typhoons. When about 30 cm tall it is ready for its final transplantation to a sunny, sheltered site. Before setting in the ground, the main tap root should be cut back by half. This encourages a wider, more vigorous root system. The young tree grows rapidly in the summer months, slowing down through the winter. During the period of rapid growth, feed monthly, preferably with peanut cake. Fruit can be expected in the second year. If fruits fail to appear or if the young fruit drop, local gardeners will drive one or two long (preferably rusty) nails into the base of the trunk about 5 cm from soil level. This is supposed to improve matters, though nobody knows exactly why. Personally, I doubt its veracity, though I must admit most papaya trees I have grown so far have received this therapy. The reason is this: my amahs Ah Ng（亞五）and Ah Lin （亞蓮）, impatient for the fruit, had always sneaked out and done the job whether I liked it or not. Even though these faithful old souls have passed on, the nail treatment has not been abandoned. I must say papayas have never been lacking in my garden!

After about five years, the tree becomes too tall to manage and the quality of the fruit deteriorates. A tall tree is also liable to snap in strong winds. It should be replaced with a young tree.

Papyrus plant (umbrella sedge) 風車草
Cyperus involucratus

This densely tufted perennial hails from Madagascar. It is a many-stemmed, rush-like plant which grows best at water's edge or even in water itself. Its graceful habit makes it a good choice for ponds or any water feature in the garden. If grown in ordinary soil, it needs copious watering—in fact, it would be impossible to over-water it. Each stem is three-cornered, hollow, and ends in a whorl of leaf-like bracts. Its striking looks make it also appealing as an ornamental pot plant. Propagate by division. In the Bible (Exodus 2:3), the baby Moses was found in a basket woven of papyrus, floating among the reeds by the banks of the Nile.

Peace lily (white sails) 白鶴芋
Spathiphyllum

Spathiphyllum x Mauna Loa

This evergreen perennial has one species *Spathiphyllum wallisii* and one hybrid *S. x Mauna Loa* which are popular house and garden plants. The lush, green, oval leaves are erect or slightly arching. The stiff flowering stems end in a dense spike of creamy flowers arising from the base of a pure-white spathe. It resembles *Anthurium* but is easier to grow. It grows best in open shade and flowers throughout the summer. Keep well watered. Propagate by division at any time.

In a study of "sick building syndrome", where the Legionella bacteria is spread through the ventilation ducts of buildings, NASA found that *Spathiphyllum* is among the top ten plants that are able to clean the air in offices.

Peach 桃
Prunus persica

Peach is a beautiful deciduous flowering tree which plays a traditionally important role in the Chinese New Year. Large numbers are sold for ornamental purposes and auspicious reasons. Culture of these market varieties is a highly specialised art which no amateur gardener can hope to match. Peach farmers toil throughout the year to achieve full flower at Chinese New Year time. A preceding cold snap in the weather helps to bring on the flowers. However, peach grows well in most gardens with a reasonable amount of sun. In full flower, these trees are a sight to behold for their delicate blooms. Later, numerous tiny peaches appear but most trees are grown only for their flowers. However, some trees produce useful fruit. If fruit are not required, a substantial pruning is beneficial soon after flowering. Peach makes more growth in one season than any other fruit tree. Unless pruned annually, a mass of long slender crossing branches will be produced with flowers appearing farther and farther out on the branches each succeeding year. Remove all weak or crossing branches and dead wood. Cut back main branches by one third. Feed regularly each month.

Peanut 花生
Arachis hypogaea

A native of South America, the peanut is, of course, not a nut at all. As a leguminous plant it is more like a pea than a nut, but even more properly, a pulse. Although a hugely important commercial crop, it is seldom grown in domestic gardens. I like growing it though, because it is such an interesting plant to observe as it develops. Simply buy some raw peanuts from any Chinese grocery and plant them 2 cm deep in the place where they are to grow. A sunny position is best. The leaves are pinnate with a variable number of leaflets. Yellow pea-like flowers are carried on long stalks or "pegs". Now here is the interesting part—as the flowers fade, the pegs burrow into the soil, and the seeds, or peanuts, mature underground. The peanuts are harvested by pulling out the whole plant. The best time to grow peanuts is when the weather begins to warm up, around April.

Pentas 五星花
Pentas lanceolata

A tough shrubby perennial producing flat-topped heads consisting of numerous, small scarlet or purple flowers. Each flower is star-shaped at the end of a long tube. The leaves are dark green, lanceolate, with a slight down. Unless kept bushy, these plants can look rangy and untidy. However, they bloom freely throughout the summer and autumn and are well worth growing at a time when not much else is in season. The plants are raised from cuttings taken in spring, or indeed at any time of the year. They root readily in ordinary garden soil. Pinch out the tips of the growing plants when they are about 10 cm tall to encourage bushiness. They are very useful pot plants and keep blooming for months on end. Old plants may be pruned hard in February but are better discarded and replaced by new plants raised from cuttings.

Periwinkle (Vinca, Madagascar periwinkle) 長春花
Vinca roesea

Periwinkles will grow anywhere

This truly robust perennial shrub with showy purplish-pink or white flowers, originates from Russia, Europe and North Africa—not from Madagascar as its name would imply. It is sometimes classified—probably more correctly—under the genus *Catharanthus*. Periwinkles are easy to grow and are found everywhere, even growing wild on hillsides or out of cracks in walls or pavements (as shown in the photograph), and may become invasive. The 5-cm flowers have an honest, simple appearance—a 2-cm narrow tube giving rise to five lobes that spread out in a flat fashion. Flowers appear almost throughout the year and it is thus a very useful source of colour. It grows well, in pots, and prefers partial sun. It is heat and drought resistant.

Periwinkle as a standard

The plants can be raised from seed from September to November or can just as easily be propagated from cuttings or by ground layering. Pinch out the growing tips from time to time to encourage a bushy habit. If required, long rangy branches can be trained by coiling wire around them and bending to the required direction. They can also be easily trained as standards but the weak stem needs staking. Tall, sparse plants should be severely pruned late in the season for new growth to appear. Alternatively, treat as an annual and raise new plants every year. Flower shops sell imported periwinkles in many new colours—blue, red, purple, etc. These may be difficult to maintain, and none does as well as the rugged local purplish-pink variety.

A point of interest is that extracts of the plant are the source of several alkaloids which have proven useful as anticancer drugs. The most important of these are vinblastine and vincristine. Both have been used to treat acute leukaemia, lymphoma and some solid tumours such as breast and lung cancer.

Petunia 碧冬茄

Petunia x hybrida

Most petunias now grown are garden hybrids. Petunias are very popular and certainly one of the most colourful spring blooms available. They grow well in Hong Kong and are equally suitable for beds, pots, or window boxes. A host of colours is available, in single or double forms, and some have a trailing habit ideal for hanging baskets and ledges. The seeds are tiny and should be handled carefully. They also deteriorate rapidly and care must be taken to obtain fresh seed each season. Failure to germinate is often due to old seed. Sow in pans in fine soil by scattering the seed thinly on the surface and pressing them in with a flat board. Sowing too deep is another frequent cause of failure to germinate. Do not sow under a glass pane as is sometimes suggested. The seedlings are small and delicate. When large enough to handle, transplant to small pots before subsequently moving to the final flowering site. A 21-cm pot will support two plants. If space in the flower bed is at a premium the plants may be grown in 10-cm pots until buds appear. They can then be transferred to the bed for flowering. Petunias should be grown in full sun or partial shade. Excessive shade produces leafy plants with few blooms. Dead-head regularly.

Philodendron 喜林芋屬

Philodendron sp.

This large genus of 500 species is native to tropical America and includes many familiar house plants. They are mainly evergreen epiphytic climbers with prominent aerial roots. A well-established indoor favourite, *Philodendron* is grown for its glossy dark green leaves. It comes in two main types, **arborescent** and **vining**. Both are easily grown either indoors or outdoors in bright shade or filtered sun. The outdoor-grown specimens can grow to very large dimensions. Arborescent varieties such as *P. bipinnatifidum* (裂葉喜樹蕉) have self-supporting trunks that grow sturdy with age. They have large attractive, deeply cut leaves, and grow well in large pots without support. The vining varieties such as the most widely grown *P. cordatum* (心葉喜樹蕉) can be grown in pots around a central support covered with bark or coconut matting. Outdoors, they can climb up rough walls or tree trunks, producing aerial roots at every node. Its growth characteristics and cultivation are similar to *Rhaphidophora*. *Philodendron* should be kept always moist, and a regular spraying in dry weather is helpful.

Note that the great favourite, the so-called "split-leaf" Philodendron, is not a *Philodendron* at all, but a *Monstera*.

Phlox 福祿考花

Phlox drummondi

This is the best known annual species. It is a sprawling plant suitable for beds, borders, pots, or for cutting. The large slender branches tend to trail, and pot plants require light staking for a good display. The flowers are about 2 cm across and are borne freely in dense clusters in shades of red, pink, purple and white. A healthy bed produces a thick mat of solid colour. Grow from September to November by sowing in pans 0.5 cm deep. When large enough to handle, prick out to nursery flats or to small individual plastic cups or pots. Transplant to a sunny site when 10 cm tall. After the plants have picked up growth, pinch off the tips to encourage branching. Requires full sun.

Pilea (aluminium plant) 花葉冷水花

Pilea cardierei

I can highly recommend this small Vietnamese perennial, both for its attractive foliage and for its ease of cultivation. The dark green, oblong ovate leaves are opposite, up to 7 cm long. They have prominent silvery patches between the veins. For this reason it is also known as aluminium plant. This is a plant for shady areas of the garden and extremely useful for plugging up odd bare areas. Small clumps look good in a rock garden. Because it only grows to a height of about 25 cm, it can be used as ground cover as well. It does well indoors in bright shade. Grow in well-drained soil rich in humus and keep well watered. Frequent pinching of the growing tips will encourage a bushy habit. Cut back plants that are too tall. It is at its best in summer and dies down somewhat in the winter when it should be heavily pruned. Plants may last two or three years, but older plants tend to become ragged and are best discarded and replaced. I prefer to replace the plants every year. Propagated very easily by tip cuttings in spring or summer.

Pineapple 菠蘿
Ananas comosus

This South American bromeliad has a centuries-old tradition of cultivation by the indigenous Indians. It remains an important commercial crop in tropical regions of the world.

The plant has large rosettes of tough, tapering leaves with spiny edges. The flowers eventually develop into the well-known compound fruit borne at the end of a short, stout stem emerging from the centre of the rosette.

An attractive and distinctive house plant can be grown from the leafy top of a fresh pineapple. Cut the top off with a sharp knife and root in potting soil. When roots have established, pot in a decorative container with good drainage. Place on a sunny window sill and you now have a long-lasting house plant that is also a good conversation piece.

Pineapple as a fruit can also be readily grown from suckers cut from an established plant. The young suckers can be planted in odd corners or on hillsides, giving a tropical look to the garden. If you do not have that much space, try growing one in a container as a novelty. Quite reasonable fruit can be obtained in about 12 months. Some years ago, pineapples were produced on a commercial scale on Lantau. Alas, nothing is left of that enterprise.

Poinsettia 一品紅
Euphorbia pulcherrima

A showy shrub, native to Mexico, traditionally used for decoration at Christmas time. The flowers themselves are small and inconspicuous, but they are surrounded by a rosette of colourful crimson bracts. The whole inflorescence is about 20 cm across. Red is the predominant colour although cream and pink specimens are also available.

The once common local variety—taller, rather leggy and of a less regular growth habit, has largely been replaced, at least commercially, by the imported bushier types most of which are semi-dwarf. The old variety was commonly seen in gardens of old homes, such as in Kowloon Tong, where the bushes grow to 2–3 m. In full flower, these shrubs are a beautiful sight. The new, imported varieties are flown in from such places as Holland, usually in a light peat medium, as air transport demands. These are practically the only potted poinsettias sold nowadays. The displays are long lasting, going on till February. What then does one do with these plants, often received as gifts over Christmas, after February?

I have spoken to many local gardeners, many of them professionals, and have come to the conclusion that there is seldom agreement on how to deal with poinsettias especially with regard to pruning and its timing. I have survived by trial and error and have the following

suggestions. In March, remove the fading flowering bracts, then re-pot the whole plant, replacing the light transport medium with good, well-draining loamy soil. Little attention is required over the next three months. On the first sunny day in June, prune hard to about 9 cm from the soil. Soon, new shoots will be produced and a light feed with a suitable fertiliser should be given and repeated every four weeks. The pots must be protected from heavy summer rainstorms. By September, the plants will be growing lustily. Every growing tip will end up as a flowering head.

The next thing to appreciate is that the colourful bracts develop in response to the shortening days with the approach of winter and the increasing hours of darkness. This development might well take place naturally, except that bright city lights and street lighting from urban development have become a confounding factor. Therefore, some intervention is needed to provide the required darkness. Beginning on the first day of October, from the late evening to the next morning, the plants should be screened from light. One way in which to do this is to drape a large black garbage bag over the whole plant. Be very careful when doing this, since the branches are very brittle and can snap off quite easily. There are obviously many other ways to keep out the light, so improvise—use whatever is most convenient for you. When the bracts are fully formed, usually after two months, discontinue this exercise and enjoy your poinsettias.

Plants cultivated in this fashion can be kept going for two or three years. However, if they lose their vigour, raise new plants from cuttings. Cuttings should be started in March, with four or five joints to each cutting. They have no trouble in taking properly.

Polyscias (aralia) 南洋參屬

Polyscia sp.

Indoor gardeners in particular will delight in this group of shrubs and small trees, native to tropical Asia, Australia and the Pacific. They have erect, multiple woody stems, often flecked with grey. The long stems, easily visible through the leaves, are an important feature of the plant's graceful overall appearance. The **geranium leaf aralia** (銀邊南洋參, *Polyscia guilfoylei*) has rounded leaves with a puckered surface and mildly scalloped edges often rimmed with white. **Ming aralia** (南洋參, *P. fruticosa*) bears long feathery leaves up to 30 cm long, irregularly and finely cut, and with somewhat crinkled edges. The foliage has the appearance of delicate fronds, almost fern-like. This is probably the most attractive of the polyscias.

Polyscias should be grown in bright open shade. They also tolerate long periods indoors. But they do not tolerate long periods of direct sunshine. Warmth in winter is essential, and if the temperature falls below 13ºC they must be protected or taken indoors. Water moderately, allowing the surface soil to dry out before watering again. During summer, give a light feeding every month. The woody stems put out numerous new shoots continually. Most of these need to be removed from time to time to prevent an unruly tangle from developing. Older plants may become too tall, in which case the stems can be cut back anytime, though always with consideration as to how new growth will shape the plant. To propagate, take 10-cm tip or stem cuttings in spring or summer. Stand in bright shade and keep just moist. Patience is necessary as rooting may not occur until after three or four weeks.

Ming aralia

Pomegranate 石榴
Punica granatum

The pomegranate is a Mediterranean shrub or small tree producing globular berry-like fruit containing masses of seeds, each surrounded by a sweet, juicy, edible pulp. This is covered by a thick, red rind. Pomegranate is one of the oldest fruits known to man, and frequent references to it are made in the bible. In Deuteronomy 8:8, a wondrous vision of the promised land is conjured up—"… a land of wheat and barley, of vines, of figs, of pomegranates, a land of olives…." It is regarded as a fruit of unusual beauty, as in Song of Songs 6:7—"your cheeks behind your veil, are halves of promegranate". It is often seen as a motif in ancient temple carvings. In ancient Greece and Rome, pomegranate was so highly regarded as to be considered food fit for the gods.

In reality, the fruit is highly overrated. The pulp is not particularly luscious, and it is difficult to eat because of the numerous seeds. It is more useful as a colourful garnish. Most gardeners value it more as an ornamental shrub, for its summer show of red, crinkled flowers on long pendulous branches. Good fruit is difficult to obtain and some ornamental varieties produce none at all. Pomegranate grows best in a sunny position. It tolerates much heat and alkaline soils that would kill off most other plants. Cultivation is uneventful and no pruning is necessary.

Poppy 罌粟花
Papaver sp.

Poppies

These elegant blooms are rather delicate and must be raised with care. All are grown as annuals in Hong Kong. The flowers have four broad overlapping petals which taper at the base to form a shallow bowl-shape. Some varieties have fully double flowers. The leaves are grey-green and deeply lobed. The **field poppy,** *Papaver rhoeas,* is the most vigorous species and is commonly found in the wild in Europe, North America and Asia Minor. There are many garden varieties of which the most popular is "Shirley" which comes in red, pink, white, often bicolour. Other species include the **Iceland poppy,** *P. nudicaule,* and the **opium poppy,** *P. somniferum.* The **alpine poppy,** *P. alpinum,* is low-growing and good for rock gardens.

The seeds are very tiny and should be sown from October to November directly in the growing site, gently pressing the seed into the soil. It may be necessary to protect the delicate seedlings from the strong northeast monsoon winds that occur about this time. Staking is not usually needed.

Portulaca (moss rose, sun plant, Nepal rose)
Portulaca sp.

The name is derived from the Latin, *portare*, to carry, and *lac*, milk, referring to the milky sap contained in all parts of the plant.

Portulaca (松葉牡丹／馬齒牡丹, *Portulaca grandiflora*) is a succulent, low herbaceous annual with a slightly trailing habit. The leaves resemble fleshy needles and the brightly coloured flowers are borne in clusters at the apex. The flowers are saucer-shaped, single or double, about 3 cm across. The double variety resembles a small rose. The most usual colour is a bright magenta, but the flowers may be red, pink, yellow or orange. The flowers appear in rapid succession but are short-lived. They open in sunshine, and close in cloudy weather and at night. Portulaca is most suitable for edgings, rock gardens, ground cover, or for planting at the base of larger plants. Portulaca is native to the warm and dry regions of the world. Water sparingly until blooms appear when more water will be needed, though over-watering encourages rot. The seeds are very tiny and should be sown in spring, directly into the growing site and then pressed in gently with a flat board. Grow in full sun. My preferred means of propagation is by stem or tip cuttings. After the summer flowering season is over, discard most of the plants, but save a few to over-winter in order to provide cuttings for the following season.

Portulaca grandiflora

Purslane (紅硬馬齒莧, *P. oleracea*), also called "pigweed", is a rapidly spreading, prostrate, sprawling annual with fleshy leaves. Its small, inconspicuous, sessile yellow flowers are borne singly, at the apex of the shoot. The fruit is a capsule containing many seeds. At one time, I looked upon this plant as a troublesome weed, very difficult to eradicate. Little did I realise that the species name *oleracea* means "relating to kitchen gardens". Only when this became known to me did I discover that purslane has a long history of being eaten raw as a salad vegetable. By all accounts it is highly nutritious, packed with vitamins and minerals. It has an interesting crunchy texture with a mild, pleasant taste—try it as a novelty in a salad sometime! Cooked, it can be used as a spinach substitute. The young shoots are used in Chinese medicine, as a "cooling" herb, but may lead to diarrhea if eaten to excess. It can also be used to prepare a poultice applied externally to relieve inflamed areas of the body. Its other name, pigweed, is appropriate, since it is used as pigfeed in rural parts of China.

Purslane spreads readily by self-seeding and layering. Cuttings take easily. Once established, however, there may be a problem getting rid of it.

Portulaca oleracea

Potato 薯仔
Solanum tuberosum

I have only grown potatoes in a small way using a large garbage bag and three market-bought potatoes. The potatoes should be kept in a warm shady place until the eyes begin to sprout before planting in October. They seem to do very well in this way and the new tubers should be ready for pulling up in about three months.

Pumpkins and gourds 南瓜類

These can be grown without difficulty. There is little distinction between pumpkins and gourds, and the terms are applied loosely. The fruits vary widely in shape and size, some smooth surfaced and some knobbly. Colours come in shades of green, yellow and orange, sometimes in bizarre mixtures.

These large plants may be trained up trellises and fences, setting the plants 1 m apart. They may also be grown up tripods, with one plant to each tripod. For those with space to spare, pumpkins may be grown without support, allowing the vine to spread on the ground. The ornamental gourds are quite effective in arbours. In addition to their culinary uses, gourds may be used as decorative fruit arrangements. If used for this purpose, they should be allowed to mature on the vine until they become quite hard. They should then be cut down with a sharp knife and dried in the sun for a few weeks. A coat of clear varnish will preserve the vivid colours.

For eating, the large, pear-shaped pumpkin, *Cucurbita moschata* (鰍圖), is what I would recommend. The bottle squash, *Lagenaria siceraria* (葫蘆瓜), is also easily grown and has an unusual waisted shape.

Sow seeds of pumpkins or gourds in April and raise in a similar way to squashes as described in other parts of this book. For best results, hand pollination is recommended. The smaller varieties may be grown in large containers.

Cucurbita moschata

Queen of the night (night-blooming cactus, belle de nuit) 曇花
Epiphyllum oxypetalus

Photograph by Brian van Langenberg

This species of epiphytic cactus takes the form of a small shrub with stiff, flat, leaf-like branches. In the late summer, from time to time, huge, exotic white flowers appear and open at about 9 p.m., lasting only one night. The flowers are exceptionally beautiful, measuring 15 cm across with pure white petals, feathery and delicate, with numerous white stamens. Its fragrance is subtle yet powerful. I would like to take a stand here and declare that in my view, this is the most beautiful of all individual flowers. That is a very big statement! Whenever my plant is ready to flower (and it has on occasion produced eight flowers all at once), I sit beside it and watch them open. The experience is almost mystical. Who would expect this miracle from a plant that, out of flower, is ungainly and unattractive. It grows well in pots in part shade, and must never be over-watered. Easily raised by cuttings of the flat leaf-like branches or the cylindrical stems.

A similar blossom, only slightly less ravishing, is produced by the **night-blooming cereus** (量天尺, *Hylocerus undatus*). This is a climbing cactus with succulent stems and a triangular cross-section which can be easily propagated by cuttings. The cactus is now widely cultivated as the source of the exotic and newly popular "dragon fruit".

Radish 葉蘿蔔
Raphanus sativus

Radish must be one of the easiest vegetables to grow, and also one of the quickest to produce results, being ready for the table in about 30 days. Almost all are red-skinned, covering a crisp white flesh that is peppery to taste. Most have globular roots but may also be elongated, as in the very popular "French Breakfast". It is a good vegetable for the beginner or for a child's first attempt with a vegetable plot since success is almost assured. Sow the seeds thinly, 1 cm deep, in the site where they are to grow. Thin the plants as the seedlings begin to crowd, keeping 5 cm between each plant. Heap up the soil around the roots from time to time. Keep well watered at all times to promote rapid growth and to ensure a crisp succulent root. Pull the roots as soon as they are large enough, when about 2.5 cm across. Old roots are pithy and "hot" and may split.

Rangoon creeper 使君子
Quisqualis indica

This beautiful woody climber has an interesting genus name which means "Which? What?". It could well be an indication of the reaction of the first naturalist to encounter this plant, when, startled by its great beauty, had to ask himself: "What on earth could this be?". This strong-growing tropical evergreen climber bears racemes of small tubular, five-lobed flowers and has simple leaves in opposite pairs. The flowers begin as white, changing to pink, then red. When in full flower in the late summer or autumn it is a marvellous display. It needs to be cut back considerably after flowering. Grow this climber only if you have sturdy support. Propagation is by cuttings. Visit the Botanical Gardens to see an example of this interesting plant.

Red powder puff 紅絨球
Calliandra haematocephala

Tropical South America is the home of this widely-spreading shrub that may reach 2 m or more in height. Its leaves are divided into two pinnae, each of which has six to ten pairs of leaflets. From November and through the winter months, unusual and attractive flower heads are produced that resemble red powder puffs, each about 7 cm across. The puffs are made up of long silky stamens which appear before the foliage is fully developed, and present a very attractive sight. It is now quite widely planted in parks. It needs a sunny, sheltered site and is suitable for containers 30 cm or larger. The branching can be quite irregular and pruning is necessary to keep it in good shape. In February, a more comprehensive pruning should be undertaken. My only reservation about this shrub is that the spent flowers do not fall off cleanly and tend to litter the whole shrub giving it an untidy appearance. Removing the dead flowers by hand helps to keep it neat.

Red shower (coral plant) 吉祥草／炮仗竹

Russelia equisetiformis

This is a graceful, sprawling small shrub with drooping branches bearing small inconspicuous leaves. In fact, the leaves are scale-like and resemble slimmer versions of the pendulous branches themselves. From spring through summer, small, very pretty tubular red flowers are freely produced. Its curving, spreading branches make it ideal for banks or for spilling over walls. Red shower grows fairly slowly and takes a considerable time to establish itself even in a preferred sunny position. Its new shoots are subject to wind damage. Propagation is by stem cuttings.

Rhaphidophora (money plant) 黃金葛

Rhaphidophora aureus syn. *Scindapsus*

Rhaphidophora—Syngonium on the left

This genus of evergreen climbers is close kin to *Philodendron*. It is probably one of the easiest to grow of indoor plants in Hong Kong. The familiar glossy, heart-shaped leaves, bright green and splashed with white or cream, can be seen everywhere. It can be grown to good effect as a climbing plant set around a central supporting pole covered with bark or coconut matting. Without support it has a trailing habit making it also useful as a hanging plant, in pots, baskets or window boxes. Grown in plain water, these plants have a remarkably long life, needing little or no care for several months. Outdoor specimens will climb up trees and walls, supported by strong aerial roots and developing progressively larger leaves, up to 30 cm across.

Propagation is by cuttings taken at any time. Pot-grown plants that have outgrown their supports should be cut back as required or re-grown from tip cuttings.

Rice 稻

Oryza sativa

Pot-grown rice

Rice? Well, why not? Some things should be done just for fun, for the sheer joy of watching what happens from one day to the next. Rice is by far the most important grain in the world and has been grown for 5000 years. It is the staple food for half of the world's population. China alone grows 21% of the world's rice, cultivating 32 million hectares and producing about 200 million tonnes a year. Even this output is not enough to feed the country. Rice is grown in flooded paddy fields, but the domestic gardener can easily grow it in a pot. Getting hold of seeds is a problem, though, since rice is not grown locally any more. Get some when on a trip to China or when visiting somewhere else in Asia. In southern China, there are two crops a year. For best results sow the seeds in the second and the sixth month of the lunar calendar. When about 12 cm high, transplant into pots standing in shallow pans of water in a sunny site. Water sufficiently to keep the pans filled with water. The plants make a surprisingly good ornament, especially around a water feature such as a pond. After four or five months, you will reap your tiny harvest, but I assure you there is no better way of bringing you back to basics than by growing your own rice. The real fun begins when you try to mill the rice you have grown. Once you have attempted this, it should be a good bet that you will never again take rice for granted, nor leave a grain of rice uneaten on your plate.

Rice: the harvest

Rose 玫瑰

Rosa sp.

Rose lovers who hail from temperate climates and who want to see their favourite flower bloom and proliferate with abandon are in for a disappointment. Rose-growing is no easy task in our unfriendly scorching summers. Most imported varieties are purchased as the bare root and potted in November. They grow well for a few years but always seem to lose their vigour. Accordingly, I must admit I am not too keen a rose grower. However, I would like to encourage the growing of a native variety, the **seven sisters rose** (七姊妹玫瑰, *Rosa multiflora*). This is a vigorous climber and very useful for arbours, fences or as "barrier" planting because of its vicious thorns. The pink flowers are produced in spring in large sprays of 30 or 40, each flower being about 3 cm in diameter and very attractive. The flowers are not heavily scented but exude a faint air of freshness. They are useful as cut flowers. Its wild, rampant habit means it must be cut back often or else it will easily take over any available space. Protect yourself from the thorns when pruning—leather gloves are a sensible precaution. Cuttings root easily when taken in autumn.

Seven sisters rose

Rose apple 蒲桃

Sygium jambos

This small to medium-sized tree is a native of Malaysia and India. It has become firmly established in the wild in Hong Kong through its ease of self-seeding, but it is seldom cultivated. In spring, cream-coloured flowers are produced, each resembling a powder puff. These go on to produce globular fruits that are about 5 cm across, light yellow, and pleasantly fragrant. The fleshy rind is quite thin and encloses a single large seed that loosens on maturity. Its taste is very interesting, being strongly reminiscent of rose water. Birds, fruit bats and squirrels delight in devouring them. So do passers-by. The fruits are of no commercial importance, but the dark green, glossy slender leaves remain attractive throughout the year and provide good shade. A small specimen in a large container makes an excellent ornamental. It is easily grown from seed and indeed any mature tree will have dozens of little seedlings scattered within the drip line. I would like to see more planting of this very attractive evergreen tree on roadsides and in our hills.

Salvia 一串紅
Salvia splendens

A native of Brazil, this shrubby plant is grown for its dazzling, bright scarlet flowers which appear as terminal spikes. There is a blue variety which is less common. The "flowers" are, in fact, colourful bracts, the true flowers being insignificant. Salvia is best sown from September to November like other winter annuals. However, a late sowing in December or even January will produce useful colour in the garden when most of the other winter annuals have faded. It needs lots of sun. The growing plants should receive a liquid feed every two or three weeks.

Sanchezia 金雞蠟
Sanchezia nobilis

This medium-sized, erect shrub from Ecuador is now quite commonly encountered in Hong Kong, both in private gardens and in parks. It has highly ornamental simple leaves which are leathery and stiff, 10–15 cm long, with prominent yellow venation. Flowers which appear in summer are multicoloured with red bracts and purple stems. It prefers full sun. Occasional pruning to keep its shape is needed. Propagate by cuttings.

Sansevieria (mother-in-law's tongue, snake plant, bowstring hemp) 虎尾蘭
Sanseviera trifasciata

These evergreen perennials are handsome foliage plants that are tough and seem to survive under any conditions. The leaves are succulent and grow straight up like long tongues—hence the irreverent reference to mothers-in-law. They are either all green or variegated green and yellow. Many have a yellow margin. *Sansevieria hahnii* is a popular, rosette-forming species with shorter, more or less triangular leaves ending in a sharp point.

All *Sansevierias* are slow-growing but require little care. Water moderately as over-watering causes rot. Pot-grown plants should be left undisturbed as long as possible before re-potting. Propagation is by suckers or by leaf cuttings.

Sapodilla 人心果
Manilkara achras

This medium-sized evergreen tree is frequently seen in private gardens but not in parks. Although in Chinese translation it means "everybody's favourite fruit", it is in reality not quite so favourite and not quite so commonly available. It is grown for its fruit, an oval, brown berry which looks much like a potato or a kiwi fruit. The flesh is very sweet—cloyingly sweet. It grows with little care. A large container will support a small tree that will provide good fruit for many years.

The sap of this tree is a resinous gum which was the original source of the base for chewing gum. This gum, also known as "chicle gum", gave the name to a once-famous brand of chewing gum called "Chiclets". It has now been replaced by synthetic gums.

Serissa 滿天星
Serissa serissoides

Serissa is a small, much-branched, dense shrub mostly used as a low hedge or as a pot plant. It has small 1.5-cm leaves, dark green, thick and shiny. The flowers are tiny, white, five-lobed, appearing throughout the summer and autumn. It can be heavily pruned to shape and size. Easily propagated by cuttings in spring.

Setcreasea (purple heart) 紫鴨蹠草
Setcreasea purpurea

This soft-stemmed perennial foliage plant with a sprawling habit is grown for its downy, lanceolate purple leaves. The stems have jointed rooting nodes and are quite brittle. The whole plant—stems as well as leaves—is purple. In summer, small three-petalled pink flowers are produced in succession. Setcreasea is a very easily grown plant which expands rapidly and can be grown in shady areas, although a few hours of sun is needed to bring out its full colour. It is best for borders but can also be grown in pots or to fill any unattractive or awkward gap in the garden. It can also be used for hanging baskets, sometimes in combination with other trailing plants. Avoid over-watering to prevent rot, and allow the soil surface to dry out before watering. At the end of the flowering season, the plant will be very straggly and should be severely cut back. Alternatively, new plants can be raised easily from 7-cm cuttings inserted in ordinary garden soil.

Shrimp plant 蝦衣草
Beloperone guttata

A small shrub from Mexico, *Beloperone* produces, in the late summer and autumn, small rather inconspicuous white flowers. These are protected by attractive brownish-pink overlapping bracts. The whole inflorescence forms a gently curving spike resembling the body of a shrimp. It is mostly grown as a pot plant. Tip or stem cuttings 7 cm long root easily in spring. Grow in part sun.

Snapdragon 金魚草
Antirrhinium majus

This is a wonderful, colourful perennial, treated as an annual, used for bedding or for pot culture. It is one of my favourite cut flowers and I am always on the lookout for snapdragons on sale at flower stalls. The great mix of colours is a truly cheerful sight. Sow the seeds in October or November. The seeds are very small and must be handled carefully. Mixing with fine sand before sowing will help to achieve a more even distribution. Barely cover with fine soil or simply tamp into the soil with a flat trowel. The seeds germinate readily but damping off may take a heavy toll. This is caused by a fungal infection. To avoid this, the seeds may be sown in a mixture of peat moss and sand with no nutrient. Or else sow in a commercially prepared substrate. To protect against infection, these substrates should not be used again for starting seeds. Water very gently and avoid excessive humidity. When large enough to handle, transplant to pans and transfer to their flowering sites when 5 cm tall. Pinching out the growing points encourages a bushy habit. If you prefer tall spikes, then do not pinch out the tips. Instead, rub off any side shoots as they appear. Some light staking may be needed for tall plants. Dwarf varieties of snapdragon are readily available and are useful for covering a large bed.

Spider plant (Japanese jumping lily) 吊蘭
Chlorophytum comosum

A common and popular foliage plant grown for its narrow, linear, grass-like leaves, white with green edging, or the other way around. It is one of the most popular plants for hanging baskets. Best grown in open shade. For most of the year, long, slender, drooping flowering stalks are produced up to 50 cm long. These stalks bear small star-shaped white flowers and small miniature plants at the ends. These plantlets root readily when pegged down to the soil. Alternatively, wait for roots to appear on the plantlets, when they can simply be detached and potted. Provide good drainage and do not over-water or the leaves may fall. Plants crowd out their pots after a few years and need to be potted-on or replaced. Its spreading habit also makes it a possible choice for ground cover.

Spinach 菠菜
Spinacia oleracea

Spinach is a winter vegetable for sowing in October or November. Warmer weather causes the plant to bolt early. The seeds are large and spiky and should be soaked for a few hours before sowing. The ground should be prepared with a good dressing of processed manure pellets to encourage leaf growth. Plant the seeds singly, where they are to grow, 1 cm deep in rows 15 cm apart. As the plants grow, thin out as required. Feed weekly with a dilute liquid fertiliser. When mature, the leaves can be picked for the kitchen. In markets, spinach is usually sold as the whole plant, roots and all.

Spinach beet (sweet chard) 君達菜
Beta vulgaris

This vegetable has luxuriant, shiny, fleshy leaves with broad ribs. It is not popular locally as it is considered a little coarse. It is easily grown as a cool weather crop in much the same way as pak choi.

Squash, bitter 苦瓜

Mormordica charantia

Easily recognised by its knobbly surface, this small squash grows to an average of 12 cm long. Even more characteristic is its mildly bitter taste which may not appeal to the uninitiated. However, having educated one's palate, it will be found to be a delicious and unique vegetable. Its cultivation is very similar to that of hairy squash (see below). However, the vine is much smaller and requires only a light trellis. Female flowers are borne on the lateral spurs which should be stopped after the first female flower. Allow no more than four fruits per plant, after which the growing point should be stopped. The young squash is quite popular with fruit flies, so keep a sharp lookout. I have had many crops ruined by these insects. Sticky traps may help. Otherwise, the fruit may be protected by wrapping with paper or plastic bags. An extract of bitter squash lowers blood sugar and has some therapeutic value in diabetes.

Squash, hairy (cheet quah) 節瓜

Benincasa hispida var. chieh-qua

This is an important and very tasty summer vegetable, growing on a medium-sized, vigorous vine. Though a fairly large plant, it can be grown successfully in a large container such as an urn or a wooden packing crate. As it tolerates part shade, verandah gardeners may also attempt growing this delicious squash.

In March, prepare a trellis of stout bamboo or other suitable material. An open metal mesh fence is an excellent alternative support. Plant four seeds at the base of each support. The seeds should be sown at least 2 cm deep in stations no less than 1 m apart. When the seedlings are established, remove all but the strongest plant. The vines are strong climbers by virtue of tendrils, and make vigorous growth. Fruit are produced from the female flowers, which are easily recognisable by having a swelling like a miniature squash at the base of the flower. Lateral spurs are also produced from the axils, and these should be stopped at the third leaf or after the first healthy female flower. The main growing shoot should be stopped at about 3 m. The squashes are at their best when 10–12 cm long. They are covered by fine hairs, hence the name. Use gloves when harvesting, as the hairs are surprisingly prickly and can cause some pain and discomfort. If desired, the last squash on the vine may be left to grow to maturity, in which state the hairs fall off and the skin becomes thick and shiny. Left in this way, the squash can grow to about 5 kg without trouble. Mature squash is identical to winter melon (wax gourds) in taste and consistency, and can be used in the kitchen in the same way. The mature squash also keeps very well for two months at room temperature.

Winter melon (冬瓜, *Benincasa hispida*), also called wax gourd, is a very close relative but grows to a huge size. It can be grown in exactly the same way as hairy squash except that the support must be a good deal more sturdy to sustain weights of over 10 kg.

Squash, silk (angled loofah) 絲瓜
Luffa acutangula

A long, slender, mildly club-shaped squash characterised by sharp longitudinal ridges along its whole length. Generally cultivated in the same way as hairy squash. Silk squash is definitely one of my favourite eating squashes. It should never be overcooked, which would ruin its crunchy texture. Left to mature on the vine, the fruit becomes very fibrous. When left to dry, it becomes Nature's scouring pad, the once-familiar loofah, used to clean bathroom and kitchen tiles. At one time available in all hardware and houseware shops, it has now been replaced by the more efficient, though less ecologically sound, synthetic scouring pad. The fruit of *L. cylindrica* are also used for this purpose.

Strawberry 草莓
Frangaria x ananassa

Strawberries can be grown with fair results but are rather finicky. Although best grown in the ground in rows, a small Hong Kong garden is unlikely to afford the space for these plants to occupy all year. They can be grown quite adequately in 20- or even 15-cm pots, one plant per pot. Strawberries require a sunny position and a well-drained soil rich in organic matter. Every summer numerous runners are produced at the end of which is a plantlet. These can be ground layered for propagation. Peg down a healthy plantlet into an adjacent small pot. It roots without trouble. When potting on a new plant, ensure that the crown is just above soil level. Buried crowns rot. If the crown is too high, the exposed root dries out. Mulching is important, especially in pot-grown plants. Ensure the soil does not dry out. Watering must be a thoroughly good soak. Flowers begin appearing in spring. For better-quality fruit, pinch off the earliest blossoms. As fruit begin to form, keep the berries clean and clear of the soil surface. Setting the plants at the edge of the pots will help the fruit to hang over the side and away from the soil. Pick when fully ripe, though some protection from birds should be arranged, such as nets. Later, as runners appear, as many as are required for propagation may be retained, but remove any others. If no propagation is necessary that year, remove all runners. To help keep the plants free of disease such as virus and wilt, strawberry plants should be discarded and replaced every two years.

Strawflower (everlasting flower) 麥桿菊
Helichrysum bracteatum

This annual species does well in Hong Kong. In spring, cheery, pompom-like flowers in yellow, orange, white and pink are produced in moderate profusion. The flowers are about 4 cm across and have a papery texture. They are highly valued as dried flowers, but make good fresh cut flowers as well. Sow the seeds in October, in pans. When the seedlings are large enough to handle, transplant to individual 7-cm plastic pots. Move to the flowering site when 5 cm high. Growing plants need full sun and relatively dry conditions. Flowers intended for drying should be cut before they are fully open, that is, before revealing the central discs. Tie in a bunch and dry upside down in a cool room, not in the sun. Sun-dried flowers are very brittle.

Sugar cane 甘蔗
Saccharum officinarum

This tall perennial grass is widely grown in tropical countries as the commercial source of sugar. The cane consists of stout, jointed stems up to 2 m, each joint bearing an axillary bud. The long, typical grass leaves have rough, finely toothed edges that are razor sharp, capable of inflicting a nasty cut. I speak from grim experience. The stem skin is very tough, deep purple in colour and shiny, enclosing the delicious, fibrous, juicy flesh. A green-skinned variety with more slender stems is also commonly available in markets.

It is very easy to grow. Tip cuttings with two or three joints are the most effective. However, simply using market-bought canes as cuttings is almost as good. The cuttings should first be soaked in water for about four days. The cuttings should be inserted at a 45° slant, or simply be laid parallel to the ground, partly buried. When the plant is established, many new canes will emerge from ground level. Do not be too ambitious—rub off the excess shoots and keep four or five to grow to maturity. As the canes lengthen, remove the lower leaves as soon as they start to brown. This will prevent the unwanted axillary buds from developing into branches.

The juice is a popular drink sold in fruit stalls. At home, it is easy to prepare a delicious sugar cane drink. After peeling off the thick skin, cut the cane into small pieces and boil in water for two hours. Some raw sugar may be added to enhance sweetness. Serve iced.

Sunflower 向日葵

Helianthus annus

Two popular types may be grown in Hong Kong. The familiar common sunflower is a towering annual growing 1–2 m high. Gigantic yellow daisy-like flower heads, 20 cm or more in diameter, are borne singly. Prominent discs in brown or purple produce edible sunflower seeds which are also very popular with birds. The flower heads turn to follow the path of the sun across the sky. Amazing! A more compact form with double flowers grows up to 1 m in height. The yellow flowers are double, chrysanthemum-like, with hardly visible discs.

Sow sunflower seeds from February through April, directly in the ground or in its flowering pot. Set three seeds together in one station, later thinning to one seedling. Grow in a sunny site in well-drained soil. Sunflower is an easy plant for children to grow. It is a pleasure to observe their sense of wonderment and achievement in producing such a striking plant.

Swedish ivy 香茶菜
Plectranthus australis

Set the scene. Washington, DC: the White House. The President of the United States is receiving a visiting dignitary in the Oval Office. They sit, one on each side of the fireplace. And on the mantelpiece sits— Swedish ivy. Apparently, this has been so for as long as anybody can remember. Presidents come and presidents go, but Swedish ivy will always have its place in the Oval Office. *Plectranthus* is a creeping plant grown for its attractive foliage and its trailing habit. It grows to about 20 cm and spreads widely. It has oval-pointed, quilted leaves with scalloped margins, dark green and glossy. It has tiny tubular lilac and white flowers. Outdoors, it grows in bright shade or partial sun, but it is especially valuable as an excellent indoor plant. Nevertheless, it needs to be taken outdoors every 10 days or so if it is not to become straggly. In winter, growth slows down considerably. New plants should be started from tip cuttings each spring. Then find a mantelpiece for it to preside over.

Sweet corn (maize) 粟米
Zea mays

Sweet corn is never as sweet as when you grow it yourself—that is the truth! There are tall and dwarf varieties, golden, white or multicoloured kernels. However, they can all be grown easily. It does occupy quite a lot of space, so it would be best to select a more compact variety. Midget varieties can be grown in containers in an open, sunny site. Sow three seeds, 2 cm deep in drills 30 cm apart each way. Later, retain the strongest seedling and thin out the rest. If no space is available at planting time, three seeds can be sown in a 7-cm plastic pot. Again, retain the strongest seedling and transplant out when about 10 cm tall. This will save three-weeks growing time for your previous crop to mature.

Corn should be put down in March or even earlier if the weather warms up. A tall crop, it is vulnerable to strong winds, but it should complete its growth before the onset of typhoons or very heavy rains. Corn can also be started in autumn.

Staking is not considered necessary for corn, especially the dwarf varieties. During growth, water copiously. The ears are ready for harvesting when the silks dry up, but to be sure, one should inspect the produce before picking. This can be done by slitting the shucks and pulling them back to expose the kernels. A plump kernel should just about explode with juice if given a firm squeeze. Should the corn not be ready, cover the kernels again by replacing the shucks carefully.

Sweet pea 香豌豆

Lathyrus odoratus

A traditional garden favourite grown as an annual vine. In spring and early summer, spike-like clusters of flowers in many colours are produced. The delicately scented flowers are excellent for cutting. Each bloom has the characteristic pea flower configuration with large laterally arising petals and central keel petals. The leaves are pinnate, the number of leaflets varying from species to species. The common climbing vines grow up to 3 m and require support in the form of a trellis, strings, fencing or chicken wire. Dwarf varieties (e.g., "Bijou", "Knee-hi") 1 m high are available and are particularly suited to small gardens. These require little or no support. However, in windy areas it is probably better to give a light support of branching twigs. In September or October, sow the seeds 2 cm deep at the foot of the supports. Soaking the seeds for two hours hastens germination. Thin to 30 cm apart. When 15 cm high pinch out the growing tips to encourage strong lateral growths. Keep well watered. Dead-head regularly, or cut for indoor decoration every other day. All seed pods must be removed.

Sweet potato 番薯

Ipomea batatas

This tropical vine from Central America and the South Pacific is grown for its edible tubers whose flesh may be white, yellow, orange or purple. Although a perennial, it is grown as an annual and is propagated by cuttings or sprouts. The young leaves are also edible. In rural areas and in China, sweet potato is commonly grown in patches of wasteland or any awkward spot not suitable for other food crops. It is often grown for pig feed. During wars and famines, this robust and nutritious plant—every part of which can be eaten—has saved many lives.

Sweet potato can be grown year-round, though for best results, start the plants in early August. It is vigorous and not particular as to soil, although a loose, sandy soil is best. It is eaten boiled or baked and makes a delicious sweet dessert soup.

Syngonium (arrowhead vine, African evergreen) 合果芋

Syngonium podophyllum

A wonderfully versatile plant for Hong Kong. It closely resembles its relative, *Philodendron*. The leaves are light green, marked with cream and shaped like an arrowhead. It makes a very decorative indoor pot plant. Outdoors, it fills empty ground quickly and can be used as ground cover. It is especially useful for shady places. If allowed to climb, it will do so with alacrity, and will then exhibit the bizarre phenomenon of changing its leaf shape as the plant matures. Later-appearing leaves become deeply lobed, with up to 12 leaflets as long as 20 cm, and turning entirely green in colour. It is very easily propagated with tip cuttings that include at least one joint.

Tapioca (cassava, manioc) 木薯
Manihot esculenta

This small deciduous shrub is becoming increasingly popular in Hong Kong as a pot plant. It is grown for its attractive palmate green and cream-coloured leaves. It requires a sunny position to bring out the best colour. The leaves fall in winter and the plants benefit from an annual pruning in February to encourage vigorous growth. Easily raised from cuttings in the spring or early summer. This plant has tuberous roots which are the source of tapioca.

Taro 芋
Colocasia esculenta

This perennial herb is grown for its delicious corms, important in Chinese cuisine and a staple food in the Pacific Islands. The dark green, heart-shaped leaves are borne on long petioles rising up to 50 cm from the ground. Different varieties produce varying sizes of corms, from egg-sized to 1 kg in weight. I have only attempted the small corms. Buy fresh corms which are most plentiful in the markets around September. These should be planted about 5 cm below the surface. They grow very easily indeed, although for best results, wet, boggy conditions are required. They can be raised in the home garden provided they are kept constantly watered.

Ti plant (Hawaiian good luck plant) 紅鐵
Cordyline terminalis syn. *C. fruticosa*

Ti plant is often listed as *Dracaena terminalis*, and indeed is sometimes known as "common dracaena". Originating from somewhere in the South Pacific, it is a palm-like evergreen shrub or small tree with papery, lance-shaped leaves up to 50 cm long. The leaves arise from a central point and are a dull mid-green flushed with red or purple. Part shade is preferred but the vivid colours do not develop in deep shade. It grows very easily in Hong Kong and makes an excellent background for smaller plants. Little care is needed and modest feeding is all that is required. *Cordylines* are very similar to *Dracaenas* in form and habit except in the flowers which are small and starry and borne in large panicles. Propagate by detaching suckers from the base or from cuttings. Both methods succeed easily.

T

Tomato 蕃茄

Lycopersicon esculentum

The tomato was cultivated by the Incas and Aztecs at the time of the Spanish incursion into South America. However, it was not until the early nineteenth century that it was accepted as a food crop in Europe.

Tomato is the undisputed all-time favourite vegetable of the home gardener. Varieties differ in shape, size, colour and flavour, but most can be grown without difficulty. They are also easily grown in pots, especially some of the dwarf varieties. "Tiny Tim", for example, can be grown in 12-cm pots, reaching a height of about 25 cm and producing masses of perfectly round, flawless fruit up to 3 cm in diameter. The pear-shaped Italian type "Roma" is also particularly suited to pots. It crops heavily and has a more piquant flavour. Gardeners are spoilt for choice where tomato is concerned. Do a little research on the many different varieties, especially the F-1 hybrids. Such well-known hybrids as "Shirley" and "Grenadier" are well worth the extra cost for the seed. Try out as many types as you can, a different one every year.

Although it is possible to grow tomatoes virtually the year round, they do not do well in the humid summer or in the misty, damp spring. It is best to raise them from September to March for consistent results. Sow the seeds in pans from September to December. When the second leaf begins to show, transplant singly into small

Tomato: Roma

plastic pots, taking care to bury the seedlings up to the leaves. Transfer to their final growing sites when 12 cm tall. For most standard varieties select a 21-cm pot at least. Tomatoes need support as they grow, and bamboo stakes should be positioned at the time of final transplanting. Staking at a later stage will cause some damage to the growing roots. Pinch off all axillary shoots as they appear. The terminal shoot can also be rubbed out if a sufficient number of trusses has already developed. Some plants are self-terminating, that is, they do not need to be stopped. If the fruit do not set properly, help pollination by spraying with a fine water mist in the evening, or gently shake the plants by hand. Feed every two weeks with a liquid fertiliser or a little peanut cake. Trusses laden with heavy fruit may need some form of support to prevent them from giving way. Fruit are best picked when dead ripe, but hungry birds may force you to harvest earlier. Pot-grown plants tend to dry out and must be kept well watered and properly mulched. If allowed to dry out too often, the fruit may suffer from blossom-end rot, in which there is a progressive necrosis of the fruit starting from where the flower was attached. Another common problem is infection with the tomato mosaic virus which causes the leaves to yellow and shrivel. There is no cure for this, and the affected plants should be pulled up and properly disposed of.

Torenia (wishbone flower) 藍豬耳
Torenia founieri

This small, compact, shrubby annual, about 30 cm tall comes from tropical Asian and African woodlands. The leaves are pale green, narrow, pointed and have toothed margins. In summer, it produces small flowers each resembling a miniature gloxinia. The flowers are in two shades of blue with a bright yellow throat. Other colours, red, purple and white are becoming available. The stamen is in the shape of a wishbone, giving it the popular name of wishbone flower. It is suitable for beds, borders, pots or window boxes, and provides a useful patch of colour in the difficult summer months. It grows in full sun or part shade. Start from seeds sown in March, although torenia does just as well if treated as a winter annual. Pinch out the growing tips of young plants to encourage shrubby growth. Torenia self-seeds readily. Since the first planting many years ago, I have never had to sow seeds again. Young plants keep appearing here and there in the garden in the early summer and can be dug up and grown on to maturity.

Turnip / Swede 蕪菁
Brassica rapa / B. rutabaga

These are not popular vegetables in Hong Kong and only imported specimens appear occasionally in supermarkets. Nonetheless they can be easily grown. The turnip is a quick growing crop, grown for its fleshy round root. The flesh is a very light yellow colour and has a mustardy flavour. The roots should be pulled when they reach the size of a small orange. The swede is a larger variety growing up to 1kg and is usually a purplish colour. Both may be sown from October through December. One way to utilise them is as a catch crop, sown in December in succession to the more usual winter vegetables. This is a sort of limbo period that can be profitably utilised by growing them. The tips, by the way, can be cut off and eaten as greens, albeit a little rough in texture.

Umbrella plant 鵝掌籐

Schefflera arboricola

This versatile evergreen shrub hails from Taiwan and can grow to about 2 m. The dense branches carry leaves with five to ten leaflets radiating from a leaf stalk. Some varieties are variegated. In spring and summer, tightly packed light yellow flower sprays appear, followed by orange fruit that ripen to purple. Mostly though, umbrella plant is grown for its foliage. It can be repeatedly pruned and thus succeeds admirably as a hedge or as a pot plant that can be clipped to a round shape. It can be grown in full sun or part shade and is valuable as an indoor plant. A larger version of this plant is the beautiful **umbrella tree** (傘樹, *Schefflera actinophylla*) which is a native of New Guinea and tropical Australia. This tree grows to 30 m with an umbrella-shaped crown and with leaves similar to the shrub but more glossy and with leaflets up to 15 cm long. In the wild, the **ivy tree** (鵝掌柴, *S. octophylla*) is a quick-growing tree widely seen on our hillsides. It has many similarities to the cultivated tree though with smaller and less glossy leaves as well as a less elegant general appearance.

Vegetable marrow (zucchini) 美洲南瓜

Curcurbita pepo ovifera

Marrows are not commonly grown in Hong Kong and only the imported variety (usually zucchinis) appears in supermarkets. They can be grown though, without any trouble. Two varieties are available; the **bush** and the **trailing** type. Both occupy a lot of space, but the bush type, being more compact and maturing two to three weeks earlier, is more suited to Hong Kong. The bush type can be grown in large pots. Marrows need fertile, well-drained soil rich in humus and may be planted in spring or autumn. Sow the seeds in April or September 2 cm deep, in drills, 1.5 m apart each way. Place three seeds in each drill and later thin out to leave the strongest seedling. Water freely. Later, attractive yellow flowers appear, the female being instantly recognisable by the immature marrow below it. If possible, try to hand-pollinate. Pull off the male flower and rub off the pollen onto the stigma of the female flower. A camel hair brush may also be used to transfer the pollen. The larger fruiting varieties are usually picked when 15 cm long before they are fully mature. However, these are being superseded by the smaller, more prolific varieties, such as the zucchini. These are picked in the immature form when 10 cm long. Zucchini flowers are, of course, a delicacy in their own right.

Verbena 舖地馬鞭草

Verbena x hybrida

A perennial shrub best treated as an annual as it flowers poorly in the following years. Most garden verbenas are from a race of hybrids that produce a sprawling low bush with attractive ovate, serrated leaves and dense clusters of flowers borne on peduncles that elongate as fresh flowers form. Verbena is available in many colours: pink, blue, lilac, white or variegated, sometimes with a white centre. Sow the seeds in pans in September or October and transplant to nursery pots or flats when tall enough to handle. Plant out in a sunny site when 10 cm high. As the young plants pick up growth, pinch out the young tips to encourage spreading. For quick ground cover, peg down the spreading branches which will root by layering. Plants can also be raised from cuttings of the growing tips taken in October or May.

Walking iris (apostle plant) 新瑪麗雅

Neomarica northiana

Related to irises, the various species in the *Neomarica* genus are native to the warm areas of tropical America. Long strap-shaped, shiny, heavily ribbed green leaves arise from a bulbous rhizome, arcing gracefully. The flowers appear throughout the summer, each stem carrying a flower with three outer white petals with the central segments having banded blue or violet markings. The flowers are very pretty, but last only a day. Plantlets at the end of these stems layer naturally as they make contact with the soil surface, thus spreading the plant by "walking". It grows without any special care, spreads rapidly, and can be used as ground cover. Propagation is by layering, although planting the detached plantlets will work just as well. Another method is by division of the rhizome.

Wandering Jew (zebrina) 水竹草

Trandescantia zebrina

A trailing perennial grown for its attractive foliage. As a houseplant, it is one of the easiest to grow. It is especially suitable for hanging baskets, window boxes or ground cover. It is known mainly in its variegated forms, green with purple edges or stripes, and purple undersides. All-green varieties are perhaps less attractive but are tougher and need less light. Its growth characteristics are very similar to *Trandescantia fluminensis*, which also shares its common name of "Wandering Jew". This latter variety has green leaves striped with white or yellow. Easily raised from cuttings. Young shoots should be pinched back to encourage side growth for a bushy plant.

Water spinach (See also "morning glory") 蕹菜
Ipomea aquatica

Green-stemmed water spinach

Ipomea is a very large genus of about 500 species all of which can claim the common name of "morning glory". Most of the species have come to be known by their own distinctive names simply because they are so different from one another. The sweet potato, for example, belongs to this group as well as the numerous beautiful tropical climbers that are more recognisable as "morning glory". *I. aquatica,* another member of this group, is a leafy green vegetable known as water spinach. Note though, that if you order this vegetable in a Thai restaurant, you will probably see it described on the menu as "morning glory". Don't worry about ordering "stir-fried morning glory"— you will not be served a plateful of cooked flowers!

Water spinach is especially valuable because it is a summer vegetable grown at a time when other leafy greens are scarce. It appears in two forms, the **white-stemmed** (白骨) and the **green-stemmed** (青骨). The former is a larger variety usually grown in water, like watercress. Its light green stems have a lovely crunchy texture if not overcooked. It can be grown in the ordinary garden without flooding but the growth is less luxuriant even with heavy watering. Better results are obtained with the smaller green-stemmed land-based variety which also needs heavy watering.

The seeds are large, hard and facetted. Soaking in water for a few hours helps germination. Sow the seeds only when the weather has warmed up, usually April to July. Delay the first planting if summer is late in arriving. The seeds are planted singly, 2 cm apart and 1 cm deep. The rows can be tightly crowded 8 cm apart. Germination occurs in about four days. Little special attention is needed except to keep the soil well watered. Harvest when about 20 cm high by cutting 5 cm above the soil. Successive outgrowths from the base keep up a useful supply for several weeks. If left uncut, the plants will begin to trail, rooting at every node. It will eventually produce beautiful flowers similar to morning glory. New plants can also be raised from cuttings but seeds produce better results.

Wedelia (creeping daisy) 三裂葉蟛蜞菊

Wedelia trilobata

You will be well advised to become familiar with this tropical plant of the daisy family because it is so easy to grow. Wedelia is probably the most effective ground cover plant of them all, and is widely grown to cover and beautify slopes. A rambling plant, it grows to about 20cm high and thrives in any soil. It spreads readily by rooting at the nodes, covering any waste ground or wall with great rapidity. In many parts of Hong Kong it has escaped into the wild. It has a wild counterpart, **Widelia chinensis** (蟛蜞菊) which is altogether a rather straggly and less attractive relative. Wedelia needs almost no care except that it tends to become invasive and needs to be kept under control. Flowering is most prolific in the summer months, but there is a year-round display of scattered, single, cheerful yellow or orange flowers, each resembling a daisy. The leaves are always green and shiny, with three lobes, slightly fleshy, toothed in the upper half, and rough to the touch. It looks fresh throughout the year. Tip cuttings provide easy propagation.

White lily turf 白山麥冬

Ophiopogon jaburan

Not to be confused with lily turf (*Liriope spicata*). This genus consists of evergreen perennials from eastern Asia noted for their clumps of slender, long-lasting, grass-like foliage. The leaves, which arise directly from underground rhizomes, are just 1 cm wide but grow in long, graceful, recurving arcs up to 30 cm long. White lily turf is best displayed as a pot plant or hanging from a wall as shown in the photograph, where the container is a traditional Chinese chopstick holder. The most commonly cultivated variety, "Vittatus", has green leaves streaked with cream, white or butter yellow. At first glance, the leaves can easily be mistaken for spider plant (*Chlorophytum*).

These plants are, in fact, not grasses, but lilies with flowers bearing more than a passing resemblance to lily-of-the-valley (*Convallaria*) to which they are related. White, bell-shaped flowers appear in rapid succession throughout the summer, in loose clusters at the end of flattened stalks. The flowers give way to dark blue or black berries. Grow in open shade and avoid over-watering. Propagation is by division.

White radish 蘿蔔

Raphanus sativus

This is a long, plump, root crop, 20–30 cm long, with pure-white, crisp flesh similar in texture and taste to the radish, with which it shares a scientific name. White radish is a fast-growing crop and should be ready for the table in eight to ten weeks. The long root requires deep, well-cultivated, loose soil with good drainage.

In October and November, make troughs 7 cm deep and at least 20 cm apart. Sow the seeds at the bottom of these troughs, three seeds to each one, and cover with 1 cm of soil. After germination, select the strongest seedling to grow on and thin out the others. The seedlings tend to rise off the ground and the troughs should be filled in from time to time to support the weak stalks. Water copiously for quick growth and to prevent pithiness. As the roots develop, they will again tend to rise up off the ground surface, especially if the soil is hard. Keep earthing up the tops of the roots to prevent a green discolouration. The roots should be harvested young—certainly well before the plant bolts.

A slower-growing all-green variety (青蘿蔔) can also be grown in the same way. In addition, an earlier start to the season may be made by planting a smaller, slimmer version of the white radish (冬瓜蘿蔔). Sowings can be made in July or August. Be sure to ask for the correct seed type for the season.

White radish is extremely popular locally as a winter vegetable and is used in Chinese cuisine in a vast variety of ways such as stir-fry, in stews and soups. It is also used to prepare a favourite savoury pudding, lo pak koh (蘿蔔糕), especially around Chinese New Year time. This recipe was handed down by my mother:

White radish pudding 蘿蔔糕

<u>Ingredients</u>
- 3.5 kg white radish
- 500 g non-glutinous rice flour (粘米粉)
- 4 Chinese sausages, chopped
- 50 g dried shrimps (蝦米)
- 250 g minced pork (or luncheon meat)
- 2 tsps. five-spice powder (五香粉)
- 1 bunch coriander, chopped
- Salt and pepper
- 2 tsps. white sugar
- For garnish: toasted sesame seeds, chopped spring onions, sprigs of coriander

<u>Method</u>
- Finely shred and cook the radish until just soft, about 5 mins.
- Add the minced pork and cook for another 5 mins. If luncheon meat is used, it should be sliced, fried, and then chopped before adding to the shredded radish.
- Take off the fire, stir in the rice flour, Chinese sausages, minced pork, dried shrimps, five-spice powder, chopped coriander, salt and pepper.
- Mix all the ingredients very thoroughly, then transfer the pasty mixture into suitable pans and steam for 45 mins.
- Garnish with chopped spring onions and coriander sprigs and sprinkle with toasted sesame seeds.
- Enjoy this with some of your home-made chilli sauce (See "Capsicum"). Bon appetit!

White radish

Wisteria 紫藤

Wisteria sinensis

A vigorous deciduous climber, wisteria is native to China and Japan. In spring, it produces in great abundance, graceful grape-like clusters of mauve flowers with a delicate fragrance. The plant is large with an extensive root system, and is not suitable for containers. It is mostly used to cover fences and for arbours. When in full bloom it provides a dazzling display. Growth is very rapid in summer and the pinnate leaves are quite attractive. Streamers or weak growths should be removed anytime they appear. In February, a hard prune is necessary, but take care to preserve the flowering buds which can be recognised by their furry appearance. Injudicious pruning means a poor display in the flowering period. Propagation is by air layering or by cuttings taken from the base of the current year's wood. It is also possible to grow from seed. Young plants are readily available from most nurseries.

Wooden rose 木玫瑰

Ipomea tuberose

A perennial, rampant, spreading woody vine requiring a lot of space. In November and December, large numbers of bright yellow trumpet-shaped flowers are produced, resulting in quite an impressive show. The general structure of the flower is funnel-shaped and similar to all *Ipomeas*. After the flower fades, the sepals enlarge to surround a globular fruit capsule containing a large seed. When mature the whole formation is brown and hard, resembling a "wooden rose". Its unusual appearance makes it a good talking point and it is much prized for dried flower arrangements. In March, the plant should be severely cut back to control its size and to encourage healthy new growth. It is most suitable for covering large fences and walls. Easily grown from seeds or cuttings.

Zinnia 魚尾菊

Zinnia elegans

An annual with a vast variety of colours and forms. The giant varieties such as "Super Giants", or "State Fair" produce 15-cm blooms on coarse 1 m long stems. On the other end of the scale, dwarf varieties are far more manageable. "Lilliput" has pompom-like flowers and grows to about 25 cm. "Thumbelina" is even more compact and has semi-double flowers. I much prefer these dwarf forms as the taller varieties are often damaged by heavy summer rains and gusty winds. In between, there is a range of different strains and many attractive hybrids which are well worth trying out. Zinnia is suitable for beds and borders and is excellent for cutting. Cutting encourages new blooms. It is also a popular pot plant, and one of the few reliable summer annuals. The flat, brittle seeds may be sown from March through July. If the spring is cool and wet, delay sowing until the weather warms up as otherwise the seedlings will sit and sulk. A sowing late in the season sometimes produces even better blooms. Ideally, the seeds should be sown where they are to grow. However, one short heavy downpour can wipe out new seedlings. An alternative is to sow seeds in small plastic pots and transplant out when 8 cm high to a sunny sheltered position. If bushier plants are desired, pinch out the growing tips of young plants to encourage branching. Dead-heading improves flowering. The tall varieties require staking. Water generously but avoid overhead sprinkling which encourages rust.

Concluding Note and Acknowledgments

To be able to garden in an urban environment is a great privilege. Farmland is shrinking worldwide. Small-time farmers are being dispossessed by mass producers and developers. They watch helplessly as the magnet of the city draws people away from the land. I frequently gain useful advice from passers-by who peer into my garden. These people—now road-workers, watchmen and other casual labourers—were once skilled farmers and gardeners, if one is to judge by the advice they are able to offer. Often I detect a nostalgia for the times they worked the earth. While it saddens me, it also makes me value all the more the good fortune of being able to garden. To these gardeners or farmers I owe a debt as I also owe a debt to my late mother Celeste, whose memory lives on in the shrubs and trees she planted. My brother and sisters shared childhood reminiscences of a greener, more luxuriant Hong Kong. My amahs (who regarded my bookish approach to gardening with disdain) taught me a great deal. My wife Nim Yin accepted (not without complaint) the wearisome role of amanuensis in addition to her usual occupation of "plant sitter". My son Brian time and again rescued me (usually with an audible sigh) by retrieving vanished script from a recalcitrant computer with a mind of its own.

I have drawn freely from publications of the old Urban Council and from the Hong Kong Herbarium. Of other local sources, the newsletters of the Hong Kong Gardening Society stand out: collectively they should be worthy of a book.

I thank Jane Ram for her valuable suggestions and Anna Yung for helping to check the accuracy of the Chinese names.

One of the highlights in the production of this book was a delightful meeting I was privileged to have with Professor Shiu-ying Hu, the world-renowned botanist of Harvard's Arnold Aboretum and now an honorary professor at The Chinese University of Hong Kong. In addition to providing me with earnest encouragement, Professor Hu, in an instant, brought an end to my years-long quest to identify "fu muk choi". This meeting would never have taken place but for the diligence and enthusiasm of Wai-keung Tse of my publisher, The Chinese University Press. T. L. Tsim deserves my gratitude for making the connection with the Press. Associate Editor Esther Tsang welcomed the manuscript in a way that made me feel like a real writer rather than a bungling amateur. Project Editor Shelby Chan proved to be a jewel. With infinite patience and a remarkable nimbleness of mind, she responded to my every need and request—reasonable and unreasonable—like a true professional. Designer Daniel Ng provided me with a huge variety of artistic ideas with the minimum of fuss so that I was spoiled for choice. Indeed it has been a most enjoyable learning experience to work with this wonderful team.

Appendices

Plant Selection Guide

Ornamentals

Vines and Climbing Plants

Allamanda, bignonia, bougainvillea, cat's claw climber, creeping fig, glorybower, firecracker vine, honeysuckle, Honolulu vine, Indian jasmine, morning glory, philodendron, rhaphidophora, seven sisters rose, wisteria, wooden rose.

Ground Cover

Aluminium plant, Boston ivy, lantana (trailing), nasturtium, portulaca, syngonium, verbena, wandering Jew, wedelia.

Autumn-Sown Annuals

Ageratum, antirrhinum, arctotis, aster, calendula, cleome, cornflower, cosmos, dahlia, daisy, dianthus, gaillardia, gloxinia, helichrysum, hollyhock, larkspur, lobelia, marigold, nasturtium, nicotiana, pansy, petunia, phlox, poppy, portulaca, salvia, sweet pea, verbena.

Spring-Sown Annuals

Balsam, cockscomb, cosmos, globe amaranth, portulaca, sunflower, torenia, zinnia.

Colour in the Summer

Allamanda, balsam, bougainvillea, brunfelsia, bush clockvine, canna, cockscomb, coleus, cosmos, crepe myrtle, globe amaranth, hibiscus, hydrangea, Joseph's coat, mussaenda, pentas, periwinkle, portulaca, red shower, torenia, zinnia.

Fragrant Shrubs and Vines

Banana shrub, brunfelsia, champak, angel's trumpet, honeysuckle, jasmine, mock lime, night-blooming jasmine, orange jessamine, osmanthus, queen of the night, wisteria.

Flowering Shrubs

Allamanda, azalea, bougainvillea, brunfelsia, bush clockvine, chenille plant, clerodendron, crepe myrtle, angel's trumpet, hibiscus, hydrangea, jasmine, mussaenda, mock lime, oleander, orange jessamine, pagoda flower, poinsettia, pomegranate, queen of the night, red powderpuff, red shower, shrimp plant, Turk's cap, yellow jasmine.

Hedges

Bamboo, bush clockvine, duranta, Fukien tea, heavenly bamboo, hibiscus, ixora, mock lime, orange jessamine, red powderpuff, serissa, sleeping hibiscus, umbrella plant.

Flowering Garden Plants that Tolerate Partial Shade

Angel's trumpet, balsam, begonia, brunfelsia, bush clockvine, chenille plant, cleome, cockscomb, cuphea, hydrangea, lily turf, nicotiana, orchids, pagoda flower, pansy, peace lily, periwinkle, petunia, poppy, shrimp plant, snapdragon, torenia, verbena, walking iris.

Plants that Should be Pinched Back

Calendula, chrysanthemum, coleus, dianthus, globe amaranth, marigold, periwinkle, petunia, phlox, pilea, portulaca, snapdragon, sweet pea, torenia, verbena, wandering Jew, zinnia.

Vegetables

Cool Season Vegetables

Beetroot, broccoli, Brussels sprouts, cabbage, capsicum, carrot, cauliflower, Chinese flowering cabbage, Chinese white cabbage, chrysanthemum vine, eggplant, kai choi, kai lan, kohlrabi, lettuce, matrimony vine, radish, spinach, spinach beet, spring onion, swede, sweet corn, tomato, turnip, white radish, vegetable marrow.

Warm Season Vegetables

Beans (various), capsicum, Ceylon spinach, Chinese spinach, cucumber, eggplant, gourds, kai choi, okra, squash (all kinds), water spinach, vegetable marrow.

Easy Plants for Children

From Seed

Balsam, Chinese white cabbage, carrot, Chinese spinach, cockscomb, beans (any kind), marigold, nasturtium, radish, sunflower, tomato, water spinach, zinnia.

From Cuttings

Bush clockvine, coleus, dieffenbachia, hibiscus, pentas, pilea, rhaphidophora, setcreasea, zebrina.

Glossary of Chinese Plant Names

In ascending order of stroke numbers of the Chinese characters

1–3

一串紅 salvia

一品紅 poinsettia

丁香花 *Dianthus caryophyllus*
    [also called 麝香石竹 or 康乃馨]

七姊妹玫瑰 seven sisters rose

九里香 orange jessamine (mock orange)

九層塔 basil

人心果 sapodilla

八月豆 string beans

十樣竹 *Dianthus barbatus*

三色堇 pansy

三裂葉蟛蜞菊 wedelia (creeping daisy)

上海白菜 "Shanghai" pak choi

千日紅 globe amaranth

大白菜 "big" pak choi

大岩桐 gloxinia [also called 洛仙花]

大芥菜 Swatow mustard

大紅花 Chinese hibiscus (*Hibiscus rosa-sinensis*)

大葉榕 large-leaved banyan (*Ficus virens*)

大蒜 leek

小白菜 "little" pak choi

小蒼蘭 freesia

4–6

山麥冬 lily turf

五爪金龍 morning glory

五星花 pentas

分枝鐵樹 song of India (*Dracaena reflexa variegata*)

天人菊 gaillardia

天冬 *Asparagus sprengeri*

天竺葵屬 geranium

巴西鐵樹 *Dracaena fragrans*

心葉喜樹蕉 *Philodendron cordatum*

文竹 *Asparagus plumosus*

日本杜鵑 Japanese azalea

日本鐵樹 *Dracaena deremensis*

月桂 bay leaves

木瓜 papaya

木玫瑰 wooden rose

木槿 rose of Sharon (*Hibiscus syriacus*)

木薯 tapioca (cassava, manioc)

比格諾籐 bignonia (purple bignonia, trumpet flower)

毛茄 okra [also called 羊角豆]

毛茉莉 Indian (or hairy) jasmine (*Jasminum multiflorum*)

毛葉腎蕨 Boston fern (*Nephrolepis exaltata*)

毛寶巾 bougainvillea [also called 棘杜鵑 or 葉子花]

水仙 narcissus (or Chinese sacred lily) (*Narcissus tazetta*)

水竹草 wandering Jew (zebrina)

火絲萼距花 cigar flower (*Cuphea ignea*)

牛角椒 capsicum [also called 辣椒 or 燈籠椒]

牛油果 avocado

牛油杯 buttercup orchid (*Spathoglottis pubescens*) [also called 苞唇蘭]

王棕 royal palm

王葉秋海棠 begonia

半邊蓮 lobelia

四季海棠 *Begonia semperflorens* [also called 蜆肉秋海棠]

四季蘭 *Cymbidium*

甘筍 carrot

甘蔗 sugar cane

生菜 lettuce

白山麥冬 white lily turf

白紙扇 mussaenda

白菜 pak choi (Chinese white cabbage, bok choy)

白蘭 champak (pak lan)

白鶴芋 peace lily (white sails)

矢車菊 cornflower

石竹屬 dianthus

石榴 pomegranate

印度榕 Indian rubber tree (*Ficus elastica*)

吉祥草 red shower (coral plant) [also called 炮仗竹]

吊燈花 fringed hibiscus (*Hibiscus schizopetalus*)

吊蘭 spider plant (Japanese jumping lily)

向日葵 sunflower

合果芋 syngonium (arrowhead vine, African evergreen)

旱金蓮 nasturtium

有翅決明 winged cassia

竹 bamboo

竹蘭 bamboo orchid (*Arundina chinensis*)

米仔蘭 mock lime

羊角豆 okra [also called 毛茄]

羊蹄甲籐 *Bauhinia glauca*

西洋菜 watercress (*Nasturtium officinale*)

西蘭花 broccoli

佛手瓜 chayote (vegetable pear)

佛肚竹 buddha bamboo

君子蘭 kaffir lily

君達菜 spinach beet

含笑 banana shrub

夾竹桃 oleander

杜鵑 azalea

杞子 Chinese wolfberry

芒 ferns

芋 taro

豆角 string beans

豆類 beans

辛氏龍樹 *Dracaena sanderiana*

使君子 Rangoon creeper

咖哩葉 curry leaves [also called 調料九里香]

夜丁香 night-blooming jasmine (lady of the night)

忽地笑 Chinese amaryllis (spider lily)

抱子甘藍株 Brussels sprouts

枇杷 loquat

松葉牡丹 portulaca (*Portulaca grandiflora*) [also called 馬齒牡丹]

波斯菊 cosmos (Mexican aster) [also called 秋英]

波菜 spinach

油墨菜 yau muk choi (*Lactuca chinensis*)

爬牆虎 Boston ivy (Virginia creeper)

狗尾紅 chenille plant (red-hot cat-tail)

玫瑰 rose

芳草 herbs

芹菜 Chinese celery

花生 peanut

花朱頂蘭 *Hippeastrum*

花葉竹竽 maranta (rabbit tracks, prayer plant)

花葉冷水花 pilea (aluminium plant)

花葉萬年青 dieffenbachia (dumb cane)

芥菜 kai choi (leaf mustard)

芥蘭 kai lan (Chinese flowering kale)

芥蘭頭 kohlrabi

虎尾蘭 sansevieria (mother-in-law's tongue, snake plant, bowstring hemp)

金魚草 snapdragon

金銀花 honeysuckle

金橘 *Fortunella margarita*

金橘屬 kumquat

金雞蠟 sanchezia

金鐘 calendula (pot marigold)

長春花 periwinkle (vinca, Madagascar
    periwinkle)

青瓜 cucumber

青豆 garden peas

青果榕 common red-stemmed fig
    (*Ficus variegata*)

非洲紫羅蘭 African violet

非洲菊 gerbera (African daisy)

非洲鳳仙花 busy lizzie (*Impatiens walleriana*)

芫荽 coriander

南天竹 heavenly bamboo

南瓜類 pumpkins and gourds

南洋杉 Norfolk Island pine

南洋參 Ming aralia (*Polyscia fruticosa*)

南洋參屬 polyscia (aralia)

垂花懸鈴花 sleeping hibiscus (or Turk's cap)
    (*Malaviscus arboreus*)

垂葉榕 weeping fig (*Ficus benjamina*)

扁豆 French beans

春白菊 daisy (English daisy, common daisy)

枸杞 matrimony vine (Chinese boxthorn,
    Chinese wolfberry)

洋金花 angel's trumpet [also called 曼陀羅]

洋芫荽 parsley

洋紫荊 *Bauhinia blakeana*

洋紫蘇 coleus

洛仙花 gloxinia [also called 大岩桐]

炮仗竹 red shower (coral plant)
    [also called 吉祥草]

炮仗花 firecracker vine

珊瑚藤 Honolulu vine
    (queen's wreath, coral vine)

秋英 cosmos (Mexican aster)
    [also called 波斯菊]

秋海棠科 begonia

紅川蓮 kalanchoe

紅杜鵑 red azalea

紅花羊蹄 purple camel's foot tree
    (*Bauhinia purpurea*)

紅桑 copper leaf

紅雀珊瑚 Jacob's ladder (slipper flower, redbird
    cactus, zigzag plant)

紅硬馬齒莧 purslane (*Portulaca oleracea*)

紅絨球 red powderpuff

紅菜頭 beetroot

紅龍吐珠 glorybower (*Clerodendron splendens*)

紅鮮單花 *Ixora coccinea*

紅邊鐵樹 *Dracaena marginata*

紅鐵 ti plant (Hawaiian good luck plant)

美人蕉 canna (Indian shot)

美洲南瓜 vegetable marrow (zucchini)

苦瓜 bitter squash

苦墨菜 fu muk choi (*Lactuca chinensis*)

茉莉花 Arabian jasmine (*Jasminum sambac*)

苞唇蘭 buttercup orchid (*Spathoglottis pubescens*)
    [also called 牛油杯]

韭菜 Chinese chives

風車草 papyrus plant (umbrella sedge)

風雨花 zephyr flower

飛燕草 larkspur (delphinium)

香茅 lemon grass

香茶菜 Swedish ivy

香豌豆 sweet pea

10–12

宮粉羊蹄甲 camel's foot tree
    (*Bauhinia variegata*)

桂花 osmanthus

桃 peach

海芋 alocasia

海灘牽牛 beach morning glory
    (*Ipomea brasiliensis*)

粉花琴葉珊瑚 jatropha
    (peregrina, violin-leaved nut)

素馨屬 jasmine

臭草 common lantana (*Lantana camara*)
    [also called 馬纓丹]

草莓 strawberry

茶花 camellia

茨姑秋海棠 *Begonia coccinea*

蚌花 oyster plant

迷迭香 rosemary

馬利筋 asclepias [also called 連生桂子花]

馬屎莧 wild Chinese spinach (*Amaranthus tricolor*) [also called 野莧]

馬齒牡丹 portulaca (*Portulaca grandiflora*) [also called 松葉牡丹]

馬鞭草科 clerodendron

馬纓丹 common lantana (*Lantana camara*) [also called 臭草]

馬纓丹屬 lantana

茼蒿 chrysanthemum vine (crown daisy)

假連翹 golden dewdrop

假檳榔 alexandra (or king) palm (*Archonotrophoenix alexandrae*)

曼陀羅 angel's trumpet [also called 洋金花]

常春藤 ivy

康乃馨 *Dianthus caryophyllus* [also called 麝香石竹 or 丁香花]

彩葉芋 caladium (elephant's ears)

淡紫百合 *Lilium brownii*

球根秋海棠 tuberous-rooted begonias

球莖 bulbs

細葉萼距花 false (or Mexican) heather (*Cuphea hyssopifolia*)

荷蘭菊 Michaelmas daisy

莧菜 Chinese spinach

袖珍葉椰子 parlour palm (*Chamaedorea elegans*)

軟枝黃蟬 allamanda (trumpet vine)

軟葉刺葵 dwarf date palm (*Phoenix roebelenii*)

連生桂子花 asclepias [also called 馬利筋花]

野白紙扇 *Mussaenda erosa*

野莧 *Amaranthus tricolor* [also called 馬屎莧]

雀巢芒 bird's nest fern

魚尾菊 zinnia

魚尾葵 fishtail palm (*Caryota ochlandra*)

麥桿菊 strawflower (everlasting flower)

傘樹 umbrella tree (*Schefflera actinophylla*)

勝紅薊 *Ageratum conyzoides*

喜林芋屬 philodendron

散尾葵 bamboo palm (*Chrysalidocarpus lutescens*)

斑葉秋海棠 *Begonia rex*

棕竹 lady palm (*Rhapis*)

棘杜鵑 bougainvillea [also called 葉子花 or 毛寶巾]

無花果 edible fig (*Ficus carica*)

番鬼荔枝 custard apple (anona, sugar apple)

番薯 sweet potato

硬枝老鴨嘴 bush clockvine

硬枝黃蟬 small allamanda (*Allamanda nerifolia*)

粟米 sweet corn (maize)

紫杜鵑 purple azalea

紫鴨蹠草 setcreasea (purple heart)

紫薇 crepe (or crape) myrtle

紫藤 wisteria

紫茉莉 marvel of Peru (four o'clock plant)

絲瓜 silk squash (angled loofah)

13–15

腎蕨 sword fern (*Nephrolepis cordifolia*)

菩提樹 bo (or peepul) tree (*Ficus religiosa*)

菠蘿 pineapple

萊豆 Lima beans

菊花 chrysanthemum

菊苣 endive

菜心 Choi sum (Chinese flowering cabbage)

裂葉喜樹蕉 *Philodendron bipinnatifidum*

量天尺 night-blooming cereus (*Hylocerus undatus*)

雁來紅 Joseph's coat

黃豆 soy beans

黃芽白 Chinese cabbage

黃花夾竹桃 oleander yellow

黃金葛 rhaphidophora (money plant)

黃素馨 yellow (or winter) jasmine (*Jasminum primulinum* syn. *J. mesnyi*)

黃葉菜心 Chinese flowering cabbage (or yellow-leaved choi sum)

黃槐 sunshine tree (*Cassia surrattensis*)

黃鴨嘴花 golden candles

黃薑粉 turmeric

圓金橘 *Fortunella japonica*

新瑪麗雅 walking iris (apostle plant)

椰菜 cabbage

椰菜花 cauliflower

楊芍藥 dahlia

煙草花 nicotiana

矮瓜 eggplant (aubergine, brinjal)

萬壽菊 marigold

節瓜 hairy squash (cheet quah)

葵 palms

葫蘆瓜 bottle squash (*Lagenaria siceraria*)

葉子花 bougainvillea
  [also called 棘杜鵑 or 毛寶巾]

葉蘿蔔 radish

萼距花屬 cuphea (false heather, Mexican
  heather, cigar flower)

蜀葵 hollyhock

蜆肉秋海棠 *Begonia semperflorens*
  [also called 四季海棠]

跳舞蘭 dancing lady orchid (*Orcidium*)

榕 ficus

榕樹 Chinese banyan (*Ficus microcarpa*)

滿天星 serissa

碧冬茄 petunia

福建茶樹 Fukien tea

福祿考花 phlox

窩菜 stem lettuce (or celtuce) (*Lactuca sativa* var.
  Augustana)

網球花 blood lily

翠菊 aster

蒲桃 rose apple

蒲葵 Chinese fan palm (*Livistonia chinensis*)

蜜瓜 cantaloupe (musk melon)

辣椒 capsicum [also called 燈籠椒 or 牛角椒]

銀竹 golden bamboo

銀邊南洋參 geranium leaf aralia (*Polyscia
  guilfoylei*)

鳳仙花 balsam (*Impatiens balsamina*)

鳳仙花科 impatiens

鳳尾松 sago palm (*Cycas revoluta*)

鳳尾球 Chinese woolflower (*Celosia argentea
  plumosa*)

潺菜 Ceylon spinach

稻 rice

蔓馬纓丹 trailing lantana (*Lantana
  montevidensis* syn. *L. selloviana*)

蓬萊蕉 monstera

蔥 spring onions

蝶豆 clitoria (butterfly pea)

蝦衣草 shrimp plant

調料九里香 curry leaves [also called 咖哩葉]

醉蝶花 cleome (spider flower)

16 or above

曇花 queen of the night (night-blooming cactus,
  belle de nuit)

燈籠椒 capsicum [also called 辣椒 or 牛角椒]

蕃石榴 guava

蕃茄 tomato

蕪菁 turnip (or swede)

貓爪籐 cat's claw climber

錦竹竿 never-never plant

鴛鴦茉莉 brunfelsia (Brazil lady-of-the-night,
  yesterday, today and tomorrow)

龍吐珠 bleeding hearts (*Clerodendron
  thomsoniae*)

龍血樹屬 dracaena

龍船花 Chinese ixora

賴桐 pagoda flower (*Clerodendron kaempferi*)

檜刺柏 Chinese juniper

薑 ginger

薑花 ginger lily

薯仔 potato

薜荔 creeping fig (*Ficus pumila*)

蕹菜 water spinach

繡球花 hydrangea

藍牽牛花 blue dawn flower (*Ipomea leari*)

藍豬耳 torenia (wishbone flower)

雞冠花 cockscomb (Chinese woolflower)
  (*Celosia argentea cristata*)

鵝掌柴 ivy tree (*Schefflera octophylla*)

鵝掌籐 umbrella plant

蟛蜞菊 *Wedelia chinensis*

羅漢松 buddhist pine

蟹爪蘭 Christmas cactus
    (crab cactus, claw cactus)

罌粟花 poppy

鰍圖 pumpkin (*Cucurbita moschata*)

藿香薊 ageratum

蘭科 orchids

鐵線蕨 maidenhair fern

露筍 asparagus

鶴頂蘭 nun's orchid (*Phaius tankerville*)

麝香石竹 *Dianthus caryophyllus*
    [also called 丁香花 or 康乃馨]

麝香百合 Easter lily (*Lilium longiflorum*)

蘿蔔 white radish

變葉木 croton

蠶豆 broad beans

舖地馬鞭草 verbena

Index of Plant Names

"The Accidental Garden" — see section "The Concrete Garden" for story, pp. 24–26.